When I Worra Lad

Growing up in a South Yorkshire
pit village in the 1940s and 1950s

Barry Jackson

Sheaf Publishing • Sheffield

Edlington Colliery

When I Worra Lad

First published in 2002 by
Sheaf Publishing Ltd,
191 Upper Allen Street, Sheffield 3

ISBN 1 85048 021 4
© Barry Jackson, 2002

*The illustrations are generally of the author's
family and relations in the 1940s.*

Contents

Yorkshire Main Colliery

YORKSHIRE MAIN COLLIERY was the reason Edlington existed. The sinking of the first shaft at the pit, then known as Edlington Main, started in 1909, and coal was struck in 1911 at a depth of 905 ft. The main seam was located in October 1912.

By 1913 a further two hundred colliers were required and wages at the face were advertised from eight shillings and threepence to nine shillings per shift. For a charge of one shilling a week, pit workers could catch the colliery charabancs, which ran three times a day – at 5.20am, 1.20pm and 9.20pm – from Cleveland Street in Doncaster. Miners were also brought from Conisbrough because of what were described as 'housing difficulties'.

Over the ensuing decades Yorkshire Main's extensive development continued. The pit shafts were found to lie in a heavily faulted area. Seams were mined in long wall faces divided into 'tub stalls', so called because the coal was hand-filled into tubs on the coal face.

1930 saw the new pit-head baths open.

A scheme for reconstruction was being considered upon nationalisation in 1947. This included the introduction of locomotive haulage, installation of winding plants on two shafts and subsidiary mine car winding gear at another. The winding gear was completed in 1953. Long wall advancing coalfaces were introduced in 1953, using conveyors and incorporating a central roadway.

By the end of the 1960s the pit employed 1,900 men, with a weekly output of 18,300 tons mined from the Barnsley and Swallow Wood seams. Forty per cent of the coal was going to the expanding market for coking coal.

During the 1950s it had been stated that the Barnsley seam, at 4,500 tons per day, had a life of 70 years – and there were yet more seams which could be opened later. It didn't quite make it. Yorkshire Main Colliery closed in 1985 just after the year-long miners' strike.

By the time of its closure the NCB owned 615 freehold and 6 leasehold houses in the area, and a further 224 homes had been built by the Coal Industry Housing Association. Today, all that is left of Yorkshire Main is a winding wheel, set in concrete at the entrance to the welfare ground. The old pit yard gates still hang on their original posts. The site is now a housing estate.

CHAPTER 1
Our House

I WAS BROUGHT UP in a pounds, shillings and pence world. A world of big flat brown pennies, of heavy silver half-crowns, threepenny bits, halfpennies, farthings with their wren, bobs, tanners, ten bob notes and big white fivers – not that I saw many of those! The money we had came from Father working at the pit, and the pit buzzer blowing caused an automatic glance at the clock ticking on the mantelpiece – it sounded as each shift changed.

It comes as a shock to realise that one's childhood is now looked upon as history. In 1950, I was a ten-year-old boy in a world quite different from today. It was only five years after the end of the Second World War and certain foodstuffs were still 'on ration'. Fish fingers, computer games, DIY stores and plastic bags hadn't been invented, and McDonald's fast food bars, jeans, electric lawn mowers, and supermarkets were things of the future.

Our South Yorkshire village existed because of the pit, everyone's dad seemed to work at the pit. My father was a charge-hand on the boilers on the pit top, and my grandad worked down the pit, as did my uncle. The boilers supplied electricity for the pit and the village, and looking back it seemed our electricity was always going off.

We lived in a house, one of four brick-built in a block – a Coal Board house. It had a wide garden at the front and, as we lived in the centre of the block, a passage ran through to the rear. In winter you could shelter in this passage and lean against the warm wall. As the fires in the kitchens backed up against this wall, the heat, from both sides, filtered through and warmed the brickwork.

The entrance to the yard at the back of the house was guarded by a high wooden gate, built between the house and the coalhouse. The cracked concrete yard had been made bigger by setting housebricks in the ground. Beyond was a large back garden with an explosion of a lilac bush and a garden shed. My dad always seemed to be building garden sheds from scrap timber, and they were one of my favourite play areas.

In through the back door was the kitchen – the engine room of the house. We washed, ate, cooked, lived, and in my father's case, occasionally slept in the kitchen.

On the steps leading to the back door stood buckets, one to fetch coal for the fire; one for water for mopping the kitchen – all galvanised iron, no plastic buckets then.

All cooking was done on the open coal fire or in the oven next to it. The kitchen range would have been black then and was black-leaded regularly. Covered in a patent blacking called 'Zebo', it would shine brightly when finished. When the old range was taken out and a new oatmeal-coloured one put in, it was thought a great improvement as it only needed wiping with a soft rag.

The floor was covered in coconut matting and on top of this and against the hearth was a peg rug. My mother had these made by 'a woman up the street'. She saved old coats against the time we needed a new rug and these were then chopped up and converted into an extremely hard-wearing and heavy floor covering. It took two men and a hernia to lift one and they were never thrown out – they had to be put down!

Coconut matting was terrible on the knees. Kneel on one for five minutes and the cross weave would be engraved there for the next hour. When the kitchen was cleaned and the coconut matting taken up, it would reveal a fine dust deposited on the floor in the familiar criss-cross pattern. With a coal fire lit all day and every day, dust was inevitable. Dustbins were literally dustbins and were so heavy the dustmen had a two-wheel apparatus that would clip onto the bin to be wheeled away.

Anything inflammable went on the fire; only dust, ashes and tins went in the bin – food scraps were used to feed pets.

In the small kitchen were crammed a kitchen chair, armchair, a drop-leaf kitchen table, the sink and the wireless which sat on top of the table.

The sink had taps set at different heights and water pipes ran up the wall, until dad 'boxed them in'.

The wireless was of polished wood, the size of a small coffin. It had a loudspeaker on the left, and a dial on the right, a row of buttons down the centre, and large knobs, which could be twirled, along the bottom. The dial had places like Hilversum and Luxembourg inscribed on it, and in the centre of the whole thing was a magic eye which glowed green and had a pie-shaped wedge on it. As you tuned in to the station of your choice, the wedge would narrow until it disappeared and you would then know you were tuned in correctly. When the set was switched on, valves as big as light bulbs would glow inside it.

Over the years the wireless was moved about. It went to the other side of the kitchen near the sink, but then in a technological breakthrough was moved to the front room. Although this made more room, there was a snag. Sound was transmitted via a second, extension loudspeaker set above the pantry door, but when the station needed to be changed, it meant a dash through the hall, across the front room and back again.

As the fireplace protruded into the kitchen, my father built cupboards between the fireplace and the wall.

On the mantelpiece – for the uninitiated, this was a shelf above the fireplace – was a clock, behind which the box of matches was kept. At each side stood a candlestick. These were used quite often, as the electricity was supplied from the pit and had a habit of failing. Also behind the clock were tucked picture postcards and other post.

The kitchen was decorated in leatherette, a thick hard paper which came about four foot up the wall. It was painted a dark brown, and if the occasion arose to strip off the leatherette, then the plaster and bricks came with it! Above this was a horizontal border – a strip of flowered wallpaper about an inch wide. Brown seemed to be the prevailing colour for paintwork. Perhaps no other colour was available.

All the doors, and the stairs were painted brown until my father had a go at flushing them. This meant ordering large pieces of hardboard from the local ironmonger's and tacking them to the door's surface. This was much admired, especially when they were 'grained'. The doors were painted cream, and then a light brown. While this top layer of paint was still wet, my father set to work with a strange array of rubber combs, which he borrowed. The finished door then gave the illusion it had a wood grain. The doors were eventually painted mushroom. Strangely, *Good Housekeeping* never featured our kitchen in their pages.

Going out of the kitchen, one arrived in the hall – lavatory and bathroom on the right and stairs running up on the left, opposite the front door.

The door to the 'front room' was at the bottom of the stairs. This room was only used on special occasions – when we 'had company' or at Christmas.

There were two sets of curtains, a light pair hung on curtain wire, and a pair of thick 'itchy' woollen ones with fringes, which hung from large wooden rings on a curtain pole.

Every house had a museum of furniture. Lino covered the floor, wall to wall, and a large carpet was laid on top of this. In 'the room' was a leather three-piece suite, large sideboard with knobbly legs, a table and four matching dining chairs, and in the corner a desk. The desk had drawers underneath and glass fronted shelves above. All the furniture was polished wood and had 'Min' cream applied to it every week and was then polished until it shone.

The obligatory mirror hung over the fireplace, which had a set of fire irons – brush, pan and poker – and a hearth plate. These were thin metal sheets which were laid on the hearth and had some kind of design printed on them. Where have they all gone?

In the centre of the sideboard was a large chiming clock which didn't work, and two tall curly candlesticks, all standing on a linen runner. Bills and other correspondence were pushed underneath this runner until the candlesticks would lean drunkenly to one side.

The bathroom was interesting, as we only used it for baths, not for washing. We washed in the kitchen for the simple reason it was so cold in the bathroom – no central heating then! Trying to wash in the bathroom on a bitter winter morning was the equivalent of a bracing dip in the Arctic Ocean, followed by a quick rub down with a penguin.

A bath was taken hurriedly – I would leap out with a towel around me and dash to dry off in front of the kitchen fire. That's one pleasure not often indulged in these days.

The lavatory was separate from the bathroom, perhaps as well, because, not wishing to waste time, I spent many happy hours in there reading.

Upstairs there were three bedrooms – my parents' room, running the width of the house, my room and the spare room. This was crammed with unwanted objects and a bookcase, constructed by my father, crammed with all my books. The bookcase was painted the ubiquitous brown.

In both front bedrooms was a large walk-in cupboard or lobby, in which were things such as the Christmas tree, and my gas mask.

I would put this on at times and wear it until the glass eye-pieces fogged up. It was rubber, with a long 'nose' on the front – a 'Micky Mouse' gas mask they were called.

Also in the lobby was a large cupboard in which I kept my Captain Marvel comics, back copies of *Dandy* and *Beano* and other comics I had acquired by swapping, and other stimulating literature, such as the *Wonder Books*. More of these later.

Going to bed on a bitter winter's evening was a feat of organisation. First a hot water-bottle would be filled and I would gallop upstairs and slide it between the icy sheets. I would put on my pyjamas in front of the kitchen fire then, gathering up my clothes in a bundle, dash up the stairs and into bed. Only a portion of the bed would be warm, the rest had to be gingerly explored with trembling limbs.

Getting up in the morning and stepping onto cold linoleum, with ice on the inside of my bedroom windows, certainly increased my speed and reactions.

My grandparents lived diagonally across the road from us and I spent a lot of time with them. They had a long back garden, which backed onto allotments. Down one side was a ramshackle shed which bounced as the floor was walked on, and hen sheds also made of bits and pieces. I spent some time 'training' the hens. I would let them out to scratch in the garden and try to pick one up. Eventually one would be captured and sit under my arm. They got used to this eventually and would sit there looking bored.

Across the top of the garden was a rhubarb patch with a strain of rhubarb which seemed sub-tropical. It was never attended to, but flourished mightily. Sticks of rhubarb were not picked but felled, with cries of 'timberrrr!' and crashes in the undergrowth. Nothing can compare with sitting on the roof of a hen hut with a stick of rhubarb in one hand and a bag of sugar in the other – dip the rhubarb in the sugar and crunch.

My grandad also had a greenhouse – another building which seemed at imminent risk of collapsing. He raised chrysanthemums with blooms as big as my head. The greenhouse had a cranky heating system which was fed with bits of coal and half-burned ashes.

At the side of the greenhouse was a large barrel which contained rainwater drained from the roof. Suspended in this was a sack of chicken manure and the resultant mixture was used in the greenhouse. Things bred in this water and could be heard howling in the night, thrashing the water as they dragged in another victim.

My grandad's idea of mending or building anything was simple – hammer enough nails in, the bigger the better, and it stayed up. Screws were just nails with a twist in them – a hammer soon had them in! All his sheds and henhuts were built to this principle, and although they looked as though they would collapse at any moment, they never did.

Grandad had a shock of snow white hair and a white moustache. He read a lot, his favourite being a magazine called the *Sunday Companion*. When drinking a cup of tea, he always took a teaspoonful first and slurped it, before drinking from his mug. He used to play lugubrious hymns on an organ which stood in their front room. All shelves, knobs and shiny wood, the organ had to be pumped with the feet. A row of stops inscribed with words such as 'tremolo' or 'bass' could be pulled out and pushed in as you wished. I would pull out all the bass knobs and, with knees thrashing the air, would press all the bottom notes together. I fondly imagined this sounded like an approaching bomber – my grandma, naturally, didn't.

She looked exactly like everyone's idea of how a grandmother should look. She was stout and wore a wrap-around pinafore. Her cheeks were round and rosy and she peered through thick spectacles – she was forever putting them down and losing them. Her hair always seemed to sport an assorted of ironmongery of hair curlers, and was clamped in a hairnet. She baked bread for all the family and there was usually a pancheon – a large earthenware container – in front of the fire with dough rising in it.

She also had some odd ideas, such as if you were wheeling a wheelbarrow at night, then you needed a light on it. Another habit of hers was to send me on mysterious missions, getting me to take a tin of pineapple chunks to my uncle's house, or a note to a woman at the other side of the village. I'm no wiser now what she was up to!

At Christmas she would produce masses of mincemeat and puddings for all the family. I would hang around the scrubbed kitchen table and 'help'. She would sometimes give me the big wooden spoon and direct me to stir while she got on with something else, and this was my opportunity to filch raisins and sultanas. I was continually told to leave them alone – because they'd been weighed – but, stirring the sticky mass, industriously, I would munch happily on the dried fruit.

Our house was always a place of such warmth. Not just physically – spiritually too. No matter how alien the outside world proved, back home with my family I knew I was safe. I'm not sure how many people would say the same of their homes and lives today.

CHAPTER 2
Edlington Village

EDLINGTON VILLAGE was not physically split in two, but even so, was known as 'top village' and 'bottom village'. Thus the Working Men's Club was the 'top club' and shops were divided into 'top shops' and 'bottom shops'.

Bottom shops included the large *Co-op*, *Maypole Stores*, *Rington's* and the *Post Office*, the library, an ironmongers, the 'lollipop shop', the paper shop where I collected my comics, and many others, all clustered around a wide road. The lollipop shop was awarded this name because it was the first to sell ice lollies. Also sprinkled among the shops were fish and chip shops – I think there were four, and these were all given mental marks as to their quality.

The houses at the 'top end' were comparatively newer than those built near the pit. In the late 1940s massive building schemes were taking place, and the Hill Top estate foundations were going in. This was a vast council estate which was eventually to swallow up the fields where we sledged, and would sprawl all over the fields between the main road and the large woods.

The village was built along the main road to Doncaster and the red corporation buses turned around and stood in our street, as it was the last stop. This was handy as, if it was pouring with rain and it was a school day, I would hang about inside our front door idly popping paint blisters on the panels, until the bus arrived and reversed into the street. It was then a dash down the street and a penny ride to the bottom village.

The school, being in the bottom village, was of course the 'Bottom School'. The 'Top School' was the Secondary Modern and the Infants' School, which shared the same campus.

My academic career started at the Infants' School just up from Carr Road, past the allotments. I remember my first day quite clearly. My mother took me to school and left me playing quite happily in the classroom. We were then taken into the hall to sing around the piano, but I adamantly refused to go, saying that I didn't like the big classroom. The teacher left me outside in the corridor. I peered in through the small panes surrounding the large central pane in the glazed double door.

Tired of this, I decided to go home. Trotting across the playground, I accelerated past the allotments, and was vaguely aware of figures behind me pulling on coats and shouting for me to stop.

I tried our front door, but it was locked, and so shot across the road to Grandma's. I was met by the astonished gaze of Grandma and my mother who were doing the washing – 'poshing' clothes in a barrel in the yard. They both exclaimed, 'What are you doing here?' Just then a panting teacher burst through the gate, explained, and took me back.

Another day, I decided to sit astride the two large heating pipes which ran along the back wall of the classroom. Inevitably, my leg got trapped between the pipe and the wall.

The teacher had a go at hauling me out, but without success. Then, the headteacher and the caretaker both tried, but despite their efforts I remained firmly stuck. The caretaker then produced a crowbar, which he inserted between the wall and the pipes, and then heaved! I was free at last – but my leg had swelled to twice its size. They sent me home with the leg swathed in a bandage and a note saying I'd been brave boy and hadn't cried.

The boys' half of the school was on the left-hand side of the building, the girls' on the right. Imagine a hollow square – infants occupied the whole of one side and the boys and girls occupied half of the rest respectively.

At the side of the school was the playground, a large dusty area with an iron fence at the front and a tall brick wall around the rest. The wall in the corner of the playground was highly polished, the result of hundreds of boys taking a run at the wall, getting a knee over the top and sliding over.

This was to get to the 'Rec', a large untidy field covered in tussocks of grass and fenced around by old railway sleepers. These had more a psychological role than a practical one, as many had disappeared over the years and gave a gap-toothed appearance. Over in one corner were weird bent metal shapes concreted into the ground. No, it wasn't the predecessor to open air sculpture parks but the remains of various rides which had long since been vandalised. I had never seen them and I was the ripe old age of ten.

In the playground were the lavatories, complete with wooden seats fastened on, and an unhealthy looking moss which grew on the unsavoury moisture which seeped through the urinal wall.

Over against the iron fence was the 'chogging' area. Chogging was a game played with marbles, and necessitated surreptitious holes being excavated in the playground surface. About six marbles were held loosely in the palm of the hand and were suddenly shot into the bowl-like depression, to try to knock out your opponent's marbles which were lying in the bottom. Those knocked out were kept.

Gambling was rife, Monte Carlo had nothing on us. Cig cards – cigarette cards – would be played. Holding a card, covered by the palm of your hand, the challenge would go out – pitch or blank? (picture or blank?). The back of the hand would then be touched by your opponent trying to guess which side up the card was.

Serious players played doubles – two cards at a time. Cigarette cards could also be flipped against the wall – the nearest to the wall being the winner.

No-one produces cigarette cards these days. Turf cigarette packets were pounced on and ripped open in the street to see if the card had been left inside. A small boy walking in the gutter with head down, scrutinising the ground intently, was someone looking for cigarette packets – thus cigarette cards and an entrance into the interminable games that ensued.

A variation of the 'flipping cigarette cards against the wall', was flipping crown caps from beer bottles. This was alright until someone discovered that the dustbins at the back of the top club were full of them. After a surreptitious entrance through the fence into the club's yard, pockets, socks, and pullovers were crammed with bottle tops. Thus they became a glut on the market and were thrown around the playground by the handful, much to the delight of boys who didn't possess any.

Serious bullying also went on in the playground. Someone once pursued me around the playground, until I suddenly whirled around and hit him in a flurry of unco-ordinated blows. I don't know who was the most surprised, me or him, but after that he just faded away. However, one boy just would not leave me alone. No matter how much I hit back, he would still pick on me. Why a boy should take such delight in bullying others I'll never know.

Through the wrestling, running, whooping, jumping, gambling and shouting masses strode the teacher on duty. Clipping ears where necessary, he would keep order, until he produced a whistle and blew. Everyone would freeze instantly, silent. Another blast would send us running to line up in our classes.

If this was the first line-up of the day, then the command could ring out, 'hands!' We would then put out our hands and the teacher would pass along the lines examining them for dirt. If they didn't pass muster the offender was sent to scrub them in the cloakroom.

Shoes would also be polished, on socks – standing on one leg and rubbing the shoe up and down the back of the leg. In those days, no-one wore long trousers until they were around fourteen years old; everyone wore short, grey ones. These were held up by cumbersome braces or a snake belt – or both. The latter was so named because the S-shaped clasp looked a bit like a snake.

There was no leisure wear then – no anoraks, or track suits, or zips – we didn't give much thought to what we wore, trousers reached just below the knees, with a thick grey shirt – no tie – and a pullover. A shapeless jacket completed the ensemble. Oh yes, and the long grey socks which could be pulled up to just below the knee. These were held up by garters, strips of elastic sewn together by one's mother and sometimes so tight they restricted the circulation. Socks were woollen then, and when they wore out at the heel they were patiently darned by mothers.

This motley collection of boys was chivvied indoors from the playground to be educated courtesy of the West Riding County Council.

We sat at two-seater iron-framed desks with tip-up seats and an inkwell set in the desk top. All writing was done with steel-nibbed pens dipped in inkwells kept topped up by the ink monitor.

The morning was usually taken up by sums, with reading out loud, writing essays, art and odd bits of history and geography thrown in in the afternoons. That was our education package.

At that time, I occupied the 'Scholarship' class for pupils deemed capable of passing the eleven-plus, who were put together and trained doggedly. Our teacher was Mrs Garthwaite, who had a large voice and a springy explosion of copper hair. She had only to slam a ruler down on the desk and thirty-odd boys would quake in their shoes.

Our training to pass the Scholarship and thus go on to Grammar School went on remorselessly. Sums were my undoing. I would wrestle almost physically with sums. My brain would go numb and I would sprawl across the desk, panic seeping into my frame as the lesson drew to a close and I still had questions to answer. I wrestled mightily – and still got them wrong. I couldn't understand it, my teachers couldn't understand it, my parents couldn't understand it. As my father could run a pencil down a line of figures and write the correct answer in an instant, it was even more unnerving. He decided that extra tuition at home would do the trick, and I would watch with hands rammed in my hair, while he went through the magic formula – and despaired.

Years afterwards, when I'd trampled through the fields of algebra, trigonometry and geometry, amazing my teachers with a total inability to grasp a mathematical concept or get a problem correct, the following was written in my report: *'Has no mathematical ability whatsoever'*. I agreed entirely, my incompetence was totally vindicated. I'd been trying to tell them that for years.

English, art and other subjects were my saviour. I could knock out a 'composition', knew the capital of various countries, could do a comprehension and read aloud, draw and paint.

Anyone good at art was allowed to execute their work standing at the blackboard and paint away at large sheets of paper tacked there. I would produce monsters with scales, wings and claws; sailing ships, sailing on a cut-away sea, which showed octopuses and amazing fish, and with large treasure chests resting on the sea bed. All this was looked upon with great suspicion by some of the others in the class.

Not all the class were being 'trained' and would stumble and jerk along when reading aloud. Reading was therefore purely for school and no-one did it at home. But as I read anything and everything it was no effort to me. Later, when I joined the library I would shove the books inside my coat so that any classmates who saw me wouldn't know where I was going.

The West Riding County Library was down the bottom village. Basically it was a large square room with shop windows, the floor covered in highly polished lino. Book shelves were arranged around the walls and 'Books for Young People', as they were designated, were in the left-hand corner. These were split into 'Stories' and 'Real Things' and 'People'.

The library was ruled by two vintage ladies in overall coats, who occupied a square box in the centre of the room, together with a small electric fire. I always got the impression that the actual library work was an intrusion on their gossiping. They would inspect the hands of small boys, front and back, and if they didn't come up to their idea of cleanliness, they would be sent home to wash them.

All the books were bound in West Riding County Council green, red, brown or grey and exuded a faint smell, a mixture of glue and paper. Inside each book was pasted a stern warning that if any book had been exposed to infectious disease, then the librarians should be informed immediately.

My incentive to join the library came from my teacher, Mrs Garthwaite or Nellie as she was known. She ruled with a rod of iron, yet got many boys through the Eleven-plus or SCHOLARSHIP – written in capitals because it was always spoken in capitals! The examination, which separated the scholastic sheep from the not-so-intelligent goats, was wrong in conception. The general feeling was that if you didn't pass, and thus went to Secondary Modern School, then your life was finished – good jobs were closed to you; you went down the pit.

My mother had the vague idea that I should work in an office and keep my hands clean. What I should actually be occupied in was never said – just working in an office was enough. The passport to this was to go to Grammar School. Both my parents were aware that education was the key to opening doors and broadening minds and made sure I knew it.

One of Mrs Garthwaite's other ideas was for us to read *The Children's Newspaper*. My mother ordered it, I read it. But it was dull! It brought a new meaning to the word grey, and I didn't read it for very long. Besides, there were more interesting things to read – like the *Dandy* and *Beano*.

My comics I look back on with great affection. The characters always celebrated various festivals in a fashion all of us dreamed of emulating. Bonfire Night editions were full of splendid Guys, unlimited fireworks, roaring bonfires, vast tuck-ins of huge toffee apples. Bangs were bigger, all rockets had pointed noses and were junior editions of Saturn V. They would readily lift hapless characters into the sky, clinging to the stick.

Easter had Easter eggs of huge proportions, Easter eggs filled with chocolates, Easter eggs rolling out of every page.

Christmas was the signal to go overboard. Christmas puddings were always perfectly spherical with white sauce on top complete with sprigs of holly. They were always being stolen from Korky Kat or Biffo the Bear and dropped on the top of snowy slopes. They would then roll down, catching the villains in the huge snowball they became.

Snow was everywhere. It decorated the lettering at the top of title pages. It lay thick in every story, falling from rooftops, usually onto policemen, who then instantly became snowmen; it was thrown with gay abandon, usually hitting Bully Bloggs/teacher/park-keeper by mistake.

Every story seemed to end with a huge feast when massive crackers were pulled. The pudding rescued from the snowball would feature in the centre of the table, with a chicken as big as an ostrich, and everyone would chortle, tuck-in and hold aloft glasses of pop. The villains, of course, could be seen through the window, gnashing their teeth.

It was only five years from the end of the Second World War but *Beano*, *Dandy*, *Knockout* and all my other favourites had seemingly never heard of food rationing.

Every child I knew had at least one comic every week, and swapped avidly. Thus I had access to a wide range of comics and swapped and hoarded them in turn with great enthusiasm. It came as something as a shock when acting as a 'reading partner' at a local school, the small boy who I was reading with didn't seem to know what a comic was!

Rainbow was the first coloured comic to be created for children and had Tiger Tim on the front cover. Perhaps this acted as an impetus for me to learn to read – I either had to wait until someone would read the speech bubbles for me, or learn to read them for myself. This comic first appeared in 1914 and 'died' in 1956.

I then moved on to *Mickey Mouse Weekly*, and I revelled in the full colour adventures of all the Disney characters.

The comics which made the biggest impact on me, however, were the *Dandy* and the *Beano*. Coming home from school I would call in Winnie Hutchinson's shop at the bottom shops in Edlington and pick up my copy of *Dandy* on Tuesdays, and *Beano* on Thursdays. They were – and still are – tabloid format, which were smaller than the other comics I had read, and had full colour covers.

The first *Dandy* was published in December 1937 and this was such a success that the *Beano* appeared in July the following year. *Dandy* always featured Korky the Kat on the front cover and inside were characters like Desperate Dan – so tough he shaved with a blowlamp; Keyhole Kate; Hungry Horace; Old Ma Murphy; Danny Longlegs and Charlie Chutney. *Beano* had Lord Snooty and his Pals – comprising Hairpin Huggins, Skinny Lizzie, Scrapper Smith, Snitchy and Snatchy, Happy Hutton, Sweet Rosie and Gertie the Goat! There was The Iron Fish; Jack Flash; Pansy Potter; Biffo the Bear and one I particularly liked, Jimmy's Magic Patch.

Jimmy was a boy like any of us, in short trousers, jacket, school cap and with socks pulled up to his knees. His trousers however were patched with a piece of material of a special virulent pattern. Jimmy had only idly to make a wish and was immediately rocketed back in time to the place he'd wished to see.

For just two big pennies each, I revelled in all their adventures every week, and I'm pleased to say that they're still going!

But there were plenty of other comics on sale too – *Film Fun* with Laurel and Hardy on the cover and including George Formby, Max Miller, Harold Lloyd and Joe E. Brown.

Radio Fun featured Sandy Powell, Big Hearted Arthur Askey, Ethel Revnell and other radio 'stars'. It was finally switched off in 1961 after 1167 issues – a victim of television. These last two comics were both in black and white.

Then came *Eagle* in April 1950 when I was nine. It was a new look for comics but the appeal for me was Dan Dare, Pilot of the Future. Much swapping went on to obtain copies.

As I got older, I dropped *Dandy* and *Beano* and took *Lion* instead. This featured on the cover the adventures of Captain Condor, once an ace pilot of Inter-Planet Space Lines, but now a convict exile on... now read on. *Lion* eventually took over *Eagle* but then both disappeared into *Valiant*.

All the comics mentioned were cheap, two or three old pence, but there were more expensive ones of 6 whole pence! These included *Superman* and *Batman*, but my favourite was *Captain Marvel*.

This featured newsboy Billy Batson who, when he uttered the word 'Shazam!', was turned into Captain Marvel, the world's mightiest mortal. Shazam stood for the wisdom of Solomon, the strength of Hercules, the stamina of Atlas, the power of Zeus, the courage of Achilles and the speed of Mercury. He was clad in a bright red all-in-one-suit with a white cloak, and had a lightning flash in yellow on his chest with matching boots and cuffs.

He did the same sort of things as Superman, but the whole thing was more humorous. As films have been made about many other comic heroes, I wait avidly for Captain Marvel to hit the screen.

I had dozens of these in my cupboard and must have given them away as I grew older. I still gnash my teeth at this – they are now worth a fortune. Whoever would have believed it?

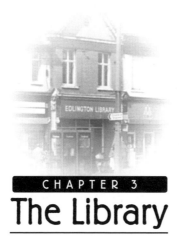

CHAPTER 3
The Library

A S THE PIPS WENT for the six o'clock evening news on the wireless, I would pull on my jacket and mac, cram on my cap and, with my library books shoved down the front of my coat, set off for the library. Few boys wear school caps nowadays – they were round with a fanciful coat of arms on the front.

Picture an evening, early in November, with fog hanging around the tall round iron street lights. This was why I was wearing the dreaded mackintosh – dark blue with a belt. I hated the thing because my mother always insisted I wear it if there was a suggestion of rain. However, fastened around the neck with one button, it could become a cloak and I would be transformed into a night rider, galloping mysteriously through the dark on perilous missions.

I would have to tighten the belt constantly in order to hold the books in place, and could estimate exactly when to do this before they cascaded to my feet. I carried the books thus, so if I saw anyone from school they wouldn't see them and instantly laugh at me.

Past the end of Baines Avenue and Thompson Avenue, past the large piece of spare ground, where the fair stopped behind Thompson Avenue's backs, past the top shops with *Crown Stores* and *Bernard's* the Barbers, past the beer-off and the *Royal Hotel*, down the slope with the British Legion flag at half-mast for someone who had died, past the Post Office, and on to the bottom shops and the library.

I would first scan the C's to see if a new 'William' book had come in. If one had, I would grab it gleefully, and then look for a second book, as two were allowed. I was mortified when I found out eventually that Richmal Crompton, the author of the William books, was a woman! Why? I just assumed the author was a man. Most were, especially those who wrote about boys.

Sometimes I just couldn't find my other book and would panic, as the library closed at seven o'clock. If this happened I would choose a book I had read before and enjoyed, and read it again.

I liked Bunkle books – the hero's name; Billy Bunter books; and dallied with Noel Streatfield, but I wasn't really interested in skating or such activities this author wrote about. Books by E. Nesbit captured my imagination – pure fantasy – and I became absorbed in them.

Back home I had my own collection of books. *The Monster Books for Boys* didn't feature monsters but stories such as *The Mystery of St. Jim's, Fred Grit – Boy Detective*, and *The Mighty Pirate*. Stories of explorers gritting their teeth and eyes, nose and ears too; of reporters who all wore trilby hats and belted raincoats and always got a scoop; adventure stories. And then of course, there were the *Wonder Books*.

These were a series – the *Wonder Books* of all sorts of things – of ships, of planes, of history for example. I usually got one for Christmas starting with *The Wonder Book of Why and What*. These had photographs and drawings explaining things that every ten-year-old was anxious to know, such as how a gas turbine works and what were the Seven Wonders of the World. I still have these books tucked away. The school stories were far from my own experience of school, full of Latin and fags; of tuck boxes; of stern schoolmasters; of dormitories; of brave lads who stood up to the school bully; tales of derring-do against tremendous odds.

I acquired books by having them bought for Christmas and other holidays, and by having them passed on from older boys in families my mother knew. Some books must have been twenty years old and had pages almost like card.

Most Sundays, I was sent to Sunday School, under protest. We were awarded book prizes for good attendance and my efforts at avoiding Sunday School were rewarded by being given third prizes, with which I was pleased. First class attendees got bibles and hymn books but further down the scale we got adventure stories.

I remember vividly one about a space ship crewed by the ubiquitous boys' school! They blasted off to Venus and fought all manner of strange creatures with machine guns. *The Adventures of a Three Guinea Watch* and *The Golden Astrolobe* were pretty tame stuff at the side of this.

One Christmas, I received a parcel through the post from some obscure relative. It was the only parcel I had ever received from anyone, and I was tremendously excited because it was the exact shape and weight of a book. Stripping off the paper, I discovered… a jigsaw puzzle! My disappointment was tangible. I found jigsaw puzzles about as interesting as watching paint dry.

I was a compulsive reader and even puzzled over the French on the side of HP Sauce bottles, and read the *Daily Herald* while I ate my breakfast. Another fascination was with encyclopaedias and other reference works.

I could lose myself completely in a book and switch off from the outside world – an ability I still have.

My first trip to the library took so long that my father came looking for me. I had started to read one of the books and my steps had got slower and slower as I made my way home. I'd nearly read it when a puzzled Father approached me and asked where I'd been.

One by one I discovered favourite authors – Conan Doyle and his Sherlock Holmes stories, led on to Conan Doyle's science fiction and historical novels. I went through H.G. Wells book by book, starting with his science fiction, then his social novels (though I didn't know what they were at the time) and C.S. Forrester and his hero Hornblower. *A Christmas Carol* by Dickens is still a favourite but I found his other books depressing. Then the books of Arthur Ransome – *Swallows and Amazons* and others – these were all read and enjoyed, some many times.

Reading has always given me pleasure, excitement, information, fun and laughter. Name another hobby that can be done anywhere, does not frighten the horses and causes no pollution. Well, all right, but I meant reading.

All this reading was a constant puzzle to my parents. My father read, but not to any great extent, but he must have read a lot in his younger years as he recommended authors such as Conan Doyle and left me to it. My mother thought there must be a medical reason for it and gave me some more Syrup of Figs.

My mother suffered from rheumatoid arthritis, and I became an old hand at visiting her in various hospitals where she underwent treatment. I had to do her dusting in the front room if her joints were bad and she couldn't bend down.

She watched my health avidly. Leaving off my mac and getting caught in a light shower led inevitably to malaria at the least she believed. I was dosed regularly with the aforesaid Syrup of Figs to 'keep me regular'.

I was almost a professional collector of illnesses. I had bad ears – so bad I would cry with pain; measles; tonsillitis; chicken pox; I went through them all and usually had at least a fortnight off school in the winter. If I didn't catch something interesting, I could always fall back on influenza. I really was ill. I'd come home, my mother would clap a hand to my forehead and I'd be despatched to bed with loads of hot water bottles and a drink of whisky, water and sugar to make sure I'd 'sweat it out'!

If I didn't get any better then the operation of sending for the doctor would swing into action. My dad would be despatched to the telephone box at the top shops. No-one had telephones at home then, and telephoning anyone was looked on as 'man's work' – operating all those buttons on the big black box was seemingly beyond my mother. I would shudder and doze, with no interest in books or anything else.

When the time for the doctor to arrive came, I would have been 'tidied' ferociously. I would lie fixed to the mattress by bedclothes straightened and tightened so I lay to attention like a butterfly pinned to a board. Doctors, to my mother, were just below God in the sliding scale of things. Doctor Ward would arrive and be ushered to my bedside. Lifting up huge bushy eyebrows, he would make his diagnosis and depart after writing out a prescription. The National Health Service was only two years old at the time, and was a jewel without price to anyone who had lived through the twenties and thirties.

I would be kept in bed for at least five days, then be allowed to come down to the kitchen on legs wobbly after lying in bed.

Crouched at the side of the kitchen fire I would stare into red hot caves, seeing tars hiss and bubble from the coal, watching dark green smoke issue from miniature volcanoes, and crunching lumps with the long poker. The long afternoons would be whiled away with the wireless. I would tune to the schools' broadcasts, to history lessons in the form of plays – with sound effects of anything from a medieval battle to an Elizabethan street. Large slabs of time seemed to be taken up by Sandy MacPherson playing the organ, leading up to *Childrens' Hour*.

A ten-year-old then was still a child, and treated as such. There were no pressures to consume, or look 'with it', no commercial pressure to buy – there wasn't much to buy!

Childrens' Hour was a great delight with its adventure plays, such as *Out With Romany*, and the *Toytown Tales*. Serialisations of books – some of which I'd read – were all pure magic. Would children today find such pure enjoyment in simply listening to such things on the wireless? It was 'Uncles' and 'Aunties' who provided the programmes I heard as I chomped my way through my tea. Large slices of home-made bread, toasted on the open fire with a toasting fork which folded up like a telescope; or boiled egg sandwiches, with a slice of apple pie afterwards, which had been baked in the oven on a plate kept specially for the purpose.

As I got well I would be allowed out in the afternoons, and I would walk quiet streets revelling in the fact that everyone else was at school except me. I made sure I was back in the house well before school came out, as other pupils would readily report to the teacher that I had been out and about.

Remedies for other injuries were various. A bump to the head was soothed with a knob of butter; a cut which needed dirt 'drawing out' was covered with Lion ointment which came in small wooden tubs with a wooden lid. It was a light orange colour and smelt lovely. 'Germolene' was used on cuts which needed healing up. Kaolin poultices were applied to bad chests. My dad would swig from a bottle of 'Kompo' if he felt ill, while my mother carried on with her record run of seeing how many hospitals she could stay in. I visited her in Leeds – a train journey away – with my dad, and we had our dinner in Lewis's; at Buxton; at Doncaster Royal Infirmary; and at a place in Lincolnshire surrounded by thick woodland, reached after a tortuous journey by bus and train, called Woodall Spa.

It's strange how a child can accept circumstances as a norm. I never questioned why my mother was in and out of hospital, and accepted that we had to visit her.

While my mother was in hospital my grandmother would supply our meals, and my dad also revealed himself to be a good cook. He could turn out Yorkshire puddings as good as anyone, and better than most.

Once better I would return to school, give the teacher my doctor's note and resume the daily round. If the weather was fine we would have lessons in the quadrangle, blinking in the bright sun. These would be handicrafts, and as my fingers had all the dexterity of a bunch of bananas I didn't make very much. Some boys were equipped with small looms and would pass the shuttle back and forth, eventually producing striped scarves. I was delegated to the task of making raffia table mats. This involved soaking the cane until it was supple, then turning it, wrapping raffia around it to gradually build up a circle. I produced two mats which were propped up behind the candlesticks on our fireplace, growing tattier as the years passed – but my mother would never part with them.

Later in my school career – at grammar school – we did woodwork exercises where we'd practise making various joints. I would end up with a hacked-about piece of wood, usually covered in blood from injuries sustained in the process. I never progressed to making useful items, such as stools or coffee tables.

This inability to do anything of a practical nature has plagued me throughout my life. Many years later when my wife came up with the bright idea of tiling the bathroom I protested, put it off, left home, came back, but still ended up in the bathroom with boxes of tiles and tile cement. I did eventually tile the room – but it took four years! Well, I kept running out of tiles, and there were never enough hours in the day when it came to doing the awkward bits around the windows.

Anyway, back to 1950! There was no sport at school, we didn't have anywhere to play anyway, but we would sometimes play rounders in the playground. The only stab at football happened when it was announced we were going out on the 'Rec'. It had not been explained to me why we were there, so when a large ball rolled towards me, I picked it up. It seems we were supposed to be playing football – and I shouldn't have done that. As the so-called pitch was on a lumpy, uneven piece of ground covered in large tussocks of grass, I can't remember the experiment ever being repeated.

No-one possessed football boots or kit of any kind, or showed any interest in the game whatsoever. It was never discussed between boys, and footballers were not seized-upon by the media like today.

Cricket was played on the street, with a dustbin lid as a wicket, but football didn't rate highly.

Thus, when I arrived at Maltby Grammar School, my grasp of the rules of football and cricket was nil. I was quite ambivalent to any sport. We would go to school, muffled against the winter blast with scarves, coats and gloves, then be expected to trot out on a draughty football field clad only in shirt, shorts, socks and massive boots.

The boots were huge, with large toe caps and three yards of laces to wrap around before finishing them off in a huge bow.

The field was always muddy, reminiscent of a World War I battlefield, and we would grow taller as we collected great clods of it on the bottom of our boots.

I hated it! The cold, the mud, the (to me) incomprehensible rules. I would pray for rain, because when it rained football was cancelled, and we could go to the school library. The library had a coal fire at one end, and, snug behind the bookshelves, I could get my homework done. No, football held no interest for me then nor any now, and that goes for just about any other sport you can care to name.

I'll try and explain. Imagine you're in a locked room, the only entertainment is a large television screen and the only programme they're showing is a lecture on Medieval Church architecture delivered in Serbo-Croat. You know something is going on, but you don't know what or why. That's the effect sport has on me!

When the teams were picked, I would hang about at the fringes of the crowd, so I'd end up as one of the 'odds and sods'. We would then have to amuse ourselves. One teacher didn't appreciate our efforts to keep warm, however, when we'd drifted off behind the air raid shelters, and lit a fire!

I remember on odd occasions I did get picked. My strategy then was to play 'full back', whatever that was, so I was well out of the action. However there was one occasion when the teacher, playing for the other side, came accelerating towards me with the ball at his feet. I knew I'd have to do something, so I ran towards him and made a vague movement with my foot. To my astonishment he continued on leaving me with the ball at my feet. I quickly got rid of it. Oh, the ball! That too was coated with mud, and kicking it was like kicking a brick.

Cricket I didn't mind – at least it was warmer during the summer. By the time the teams were picked, padded up, fielders distributed, and we'd had a couple of overs, the lesson was over anyway. I'd pick a spot as far away from the action as possible, as usual, and chat to a couple of like-minded souls.

Another feature of summer would be boys rushing up to you and asking in anxious tones, 'What's the score', as though the fate of the world hung on it. They were alluding to some interminable Test Match, I believe.

Athletics I didn't mind, as I discovered I was quite good at both the high and long jump, and I was also all right at cross-country running.

I have continued with a total disinterest in any sporting activity. I still have no idea of the rules of football or cricket. To make matters worse, my wife and daughter are both keen football supporters, home and away!

My list of boring spectator sports is endless, and probably starts with motor racing and golf. But one thought sustains me – I am not alone! Yes, I've discovered there are others out there who, like me, have no interest in sport whatsoever. Perhaps we should get together and form a team?

I suppose, these days, educationalists would raise eyebrows at our lack of sporting and 'cultural' interests. We didn't have swimming lessons or educational visits; there were certainly no holidays arranged by the school or trips to local museums or places of interest. A lot of families probably wouldn't have been able to afford to pay anyway. Some boys would come to school in pumps – canvas shoes with rubber soles – whatever the weather, others had their heads and faces painted in a bright purple substance (a treatment for ringworm), but we accepted these things and it never bothered us.

Mrs Garthwaite, however, would arrange trips to such places as the far metropolis of Sheffield to see a pantomime at the *Lyceum*. And somehow she fiddled it so that no-one in the class was left out.

As I industriously polished my shoes each evening with the radio playing and the fire falling softly in the grate, my father would always say, 'Your clothes might sometimes be shabby, but your shoes can always be clean'.

CHAPTER 4
Our Street

T HE DOCTOR'S CAR was one of the few which used our street. No-one owned cars and the street was used as a playground. We moved to one side when anything passed and resumed our games when it had gone. The only other vehicles were delivery vans or lorries, from the *Co-op* or home coal delivery service for instance.

The *Rington's Tea* van was always of interest. It was driven by some mysterious means which meant a chain whirled around underneath the vehicle. This could only be seen if you were lying flat on your stomach. Thus, the driver would trundle down the street, passing groups of kids who would immediately throw themselves flat on the pavement to get a look at the chain; I wonder if he caught on why we were doing it – prostrating ourselves like heathens before some pagan god. A *Rington's Tea* van could hardly be classed as an object of reverence.

The *Co-op* van would deliver groceries in stout cardboard boxes on Friday evenings. One of my regular jobs would be to take the order back again on the Saturday as they invariably got it wrong.

In summer, *Masserella's* two-wheeled, horsedrawn ice-cream carts would meander down the street. They had a roof supported by barley sugar twist pillars, and were decorated with floral lettering. Underneath the roof were paintings of local beauty spots, such as 'The Dell, Hexthorpe' and 'The Weir, Sprotbrough'. I wonder where they've gone. Are they mouldering forgotten in some barn, or have they been meticulously restored and preserved?

The coal lorry was a regular visitor – a tip-up one with a partition across the centre, a ton of coal in each section. It would tip the coal half on and half off the pavement before going on to the next house on the list with tail-gate swinging.

If you had a wheelbarrow, and were able, the coal would be trundled around to the back yard. The village was toured by lugubrious characters who would get it in for you. Their charge was around three old shillings (15p) or alternatively a barrow-load of coal.

The coal was looked at critically. There could be a lot of slack – small powdery coal, bats – pieces of stone which had not been winkled out, or cobbles – pieces of coal as large as a man's fist. Mixed up in all this would be lumps as big as a man's chest which would have to be attacked with a coal hammer before they were any use. These could also be used to form walls behind which the smaller coal could be piled, either in the coal house or the yard. My grandad would take a large lump, lob it expertly underhand on to the fire, then gripping the mantleshelf with both hands for balance, crush it down onto the fire with his boots. A lump like this could last for hours and they were used, mainly, if you were going out and wanted the fire to be in when you got back.

Slack was also used for the same purpose. The fire would be completely smothered by the small coal until only a steady trickle of smoke would tell you it was still burning. A jab with the poker when you came back, and it would burst into brilliant flame.

The fire was of great importance. It was the sole means of cooking, heating and hotting up the water by means of the back boiler. Lighting the fire was an art. My dad used to bring off-cuts from the joiners' shop at the pit, and these would be chopped into sticks on the back step. We kept a large box in the pantry full of sticks and these would be replenished daily so that we wouldn't run out.

I became quite good at chopping sticks. Holding the wood steady with my left hand, I would bring the axe smartly down, splitting the wood along the grain in a series of quick movements.

One of the last things my dad did before going to bed was to throw a handful of sticks on to the hob on top of the oven with a chunk. Thus they would be tinder dry in the morning. They could also be used to build forts – being roughly square, they could be made into buildings on the fireplace.

To light a fire, newspaper would be crumpled in the fireplace and a wigwam of sticks built around it. Lighting the paper, small pieces of coal would be rapidly and delicately stacked around the sticks, then larger pieces as the fire spread.

To make the fire burn more fiercely, a piece of thin metal with a handle on, like a knight's shield, would be propped in front of the fire to make it draw. To make it go even harder a newspaper would also be held around the fire and shield, until the paper turned brown and smouldered. The fire would roar up the chimney at this attention, and was soon burning well.

If an ambulance went down the street it was automatic that you held your collar until you saw a dog – it was bad luck to do otherwise. Also it was firmly believed that if you played near a grid (grate) then you would inevitably catch a fever and be carted off to the fever hospital.

When it was very hot we would sometimes sit on the kerb, with knees under our chin and, with lollipop sticks, dig at the soft tar oozing from the road surface. Totally absorbed, a row of scruffy kids sat, all with a soft lump of tar on the end of a stick.

There was great delight if the road or footpath was to be resurfaced. A man in a tar-stiff apron and goggles would swing a long nozzle back and forth, coating the pavement or road in a black, steaming, glistening coat. The spray of hot tar came from a tar-streaked boiler on iron wheels which would be towed slowly up the road. A fire was fed from the other end and a stove-pipe chimney carried away the smoke. We watched all of this avidly and with great fascination.

Large barrels would be swung up on to the boiler by a pulley device and the bung knocked out. The tar would pour into the boiler in long slow 'gloops'. As the spray progressed up the road, a lorry filled with pebbles would slowly reverse after it, and a couple of men with shovels would scrape the pebbles down, and with a deft flick of the wrist, spread them in a fan over the hot tar. Bringing up the rear, a man with a stiff brush covered up bits the others had missed. A road roller would crunch and chuff behind, pressing down the pebbles with its great fly wheel continually spinning.

All this equipment would be stored for the night on a piece of waste-land near the bottom of the street called 'the triangle'. (Its shape was created by two roads meeting at an angle.)

There would be a hut on iron wheels, a large coke brazier with a kettle on top; lorries; tar barrels and a large wooden box containing tools, all guarded by a night-watchman.

Despite the night-watchman someone knocked out a bung from one of the barrels causing the tar to escape. For years afterwards, in very hot weather, the ground where the tar had spread would give underfoot.

The road was resurfaced one year in a smooth, black tarmac and was rapidly found to be ideal for chalking on.

A front garden further up the street had a huge rockery made of large, carefully arranged, stones. These were a kind of quartz and, when smashed on the pavement, shattered into flat crystal-like pieces that made an ideal substitute for chalk.

One of these lumps was duly obtained, smashed, and each child set to work. With little traffic around, we knelt on the road and drew. There were battleships shooting massive shells, and ladies, four-foot tall in long ball gowns, elaborately decorated, planes roared from one side of the road to the other and matchstick men ran riot. There were ships with sails billowing, comic faces leering, houses with paths, flowers and chimneys puffing smoke.

The street was quiet, all the boys and girls were absorbed in these creations. The drawings joined, intertwined; three or more at a time would co-operate on a large drawing.

We created a huge, violent, wonderful design which went from one side of the road to the other, and spread up and down the slight slope. Outraged housewives ended our fun – with buckets of water thrown on the road and brushes wielded. We often drew again, but never creating such a huge combined mural. Our work sparkled all too briefly on a dusty road in a South Yorkshire pit village – an artistic expression, started in a moment and absorbing a street full of kids for a long afternoon.

Half way along the length of our street the houses were set further back, so the road widened, then narrowed again, forming what we called 'the square'. It was here we played ball games which needed more space. Cricket was a favourite. We'd borrow a dustbin lid and prop it up on a brick. Someone would provide a bat.

Usually an old threadbare tennis ball was used, but once someone managed to obtain an old cricket ball. Admittedly, all the red coating had gone, and it was somewhat chipped and scarred, but it was a *real* cricket ball. The only snag was, on this occasion, we didn't have a bat! We made one by the simple expedient of obtaining a short plank and sawing a handle at one end.

We played cricket to rules which would have staggered the MCC. For instance, no slogging; and you were out if you hit a ball into a garden. Everyone played for themselves – no teams were ever picked – and runs were scored by running between the dustbin-lid wicket and a brick, which marked the bowler's point. 'Walking back' would be shouted if it were seen that another run couldn't be scored without being stumped. 'Running back to save time' was also a familiar cry. The order of batting was decided by telling foggy, seggy, thirdy, etc. (first, second, third and so on).

I was first in to bat on this occasion. I took my place at the crease and with a keen eye scanned the field. The bowler ran up and delivered the ball underhand, I stepped forward and hit the ball hard, fair and square.

It felt as though the bat had been plugged into the mains. The vibration hit my hands, and rippled up my arms causing me to drop the plank bat from numb and nerveless fingers. My cap shot six feet into the air and my socks abruptly dropped around my ankles. So that's why bats are made with blade and handle from separate pieces!

The ball had trickled down the pitch and the call of 'cars coming' made us remove the dustbin lid and bricks. A car passed, its headlights set on top of the mud guards, and running boards that swept along its length at each side — it was black of course.

When not playing on the street we would play in someone's garden. A certain boy's garden was used for digging holes — a wonderful pursuit, especially if filled with water or roofed over to form a dug-out. Candles would then be filched and lit so we could sit inside these holes.

We also made huts from loose planks which had the habit of collapsing at any given moment — which added to the spice of being inside when they did. Fires were another pursuit — just lighting one and keeping it going would occupy us for a morning and would use up any paper, cardboard or old wood for yards around. Once, one of these fires got out of control and with amazing speed spread through dry grass and began to crackle hungrily around a garden fence. Our ineffectual and panic-stricken efforts to put out the blaze were soon re-inforced by some judicious buckets of water from parents who then told us not to do it again. However, it was put more colourfully than that.

We would also meet in our garden shed and form societies with passwords and secret rules. We had secret knocks that allowed you to enter the headquarters. All this came to nought when someone's elder sister, ignorant of all these restrictions, wrenched open the door to take someone off for their dinner.

I also possessed a tent and, if the weather was fine, pitched it on the lawn in the back garden. The grass would have had to be scythed down first, and the admission to this glamorous world was to bring a bundle of comics. With bottles of cream soda and with tent flap securely threaded, we would swig the fizzy liquid and happily browse through the comic world.

The smells would be of cut grass and hot canvas; of garden mint and dinner cooking — we occupied a very tight but warm and safe world.

There was no sex or drugs or designer clothes or television heroes. Just the buzz of a passing bee and the sweltering air of a thick canvas tent, sagging on a piece of rough grass.

CHAPTER 5

Play

GAMES IN THE STREET ran in 'seasons'. Not the spring or summer, but 'seasons' when suddenly everyone would be playing a particular game. A curious telepathy meant that no-one decided when we played whip-and-top, for instance, but suddenly everyone would be playing it.

Armed with a whip with a leather thong, and a top, I would wind the thong tightly around the top. Carefully holding it upright with the right knee, I would jerk it, setting the top spinning. Then with left hand on left knee, I would whip the top to keep it going.

There were two types of top, the conventional type and 'winda brekkers'. These were mushroom shaped and would jump with a crack when hit by the whip – thus the legend that they could break windows.

The head of the tops would be chalked on in various colours so they merged and changed when spinning. Girls did this more than boys and would spend more time carefully colouring the tops than actually whipping them.

Then came a craze for trolleys – or soap boxes on wheels. I cadged an old pushchair from my Auntie Margaret and soon bored with pushing it home, I sat on it, careering into hedge and kerb as it traced an erratic course, braking it with my feet.

I sawed off the wheels and axles and nagged my dad until he nailed together a flat bed. We fixed the back wheels on, then came the piece which stuck out at the front to carry the steering arm. The poker was pushed into the fire then, when glowing, was pushed through the two pieces of wood to take a long nut and bolt – no electric drills in those days.

Shaking out rusty tins from the shed, we found a nut and bolt that would fit, plus some washers, and it was bolted together. A piece of discarded washing line later, and I was running up the passage, towing it into the street.

As our street had a slight slope, we would sit side-saddle on the trolley, pushing it up the street with the right leg before crouching on it and rolling down. I once set off and found myself going too fast. I began to steer in a series of loops, but it continued to get faster. As the main road was rapidly approaching, I tried to turn it, but flipped over, and I found myself on my back in the road with the trolley, upside down, feet away, its wheels spinning.

Girls would play skipping games, twirling a long piece of rope across the street, hitting the road with a steady slap. The rhymes to these skipping games seemed endless:

Jeremiah poked the fire
Puff, Puff, Puff, PUFF

You-are-out, they would chant, while girls ran into the rope, skipped, and ran out again. Sometimes they would do this two at a time, and we would also join in, much to the girls' annoyance.

To start a game when someone had to be 'on' an elaborate series of ways of picking that person went on:

One potato, two potato, three potato, four
Five potato, six potato, seven potato, more.

Or:

Eeny, meeny, miney, mo
Sit a baby on the po
When it's done,
Wipe its bum,
Eeny meeny, miney, mo.

Thus, someone would be picked for 'tiggy', for instance, which would be elaborated as 'Tiggy off ground', when you couldn't be tigged if you had leapt up on a wall. Long arguments went on if a person had stood on a brick, and this was deemed by the person who was 'on' that the other was not off the ground.

'Hot rye' was a game we all enjoyed. A circle would be formed and everyone would stand with their legs astride, and feet touching. A ball would be dropped into the centre of the circle and the legs of the person it rolled through was 'on'. As soon as that happened, everyone would scatter instantly. It was then the selected person's role to pick up the ball and try to hit someone with it. Thus, as you were hit, you too became 'on'. And so it proceeded until just one person was left to dodge the ball, rapidly thrown from hand to hand. You could, however, defend yourself with clenched fists.

Another favourite game was 'Hiddy' – Hide and Seek. A spot was picked, called 'the block', someone was selected to be 'on', and everyone would gallop off to hide. The child who was 'on' would then count up to five hundred in fives, with head down and eyes closed. When five hundred was reached, he or she would shout, 'Coming, ready or not'. It was then up to everyone to get to the spot and hit it with their hand and shout, 'Blocko, one, two, three' before the person who was 'on' got back to the block.

We hid behind walls, down jennels, up trees. On one occasion, I found a particularly good spot. I discovered that privet hedges growing against walls formed a kind of tunnel between their stems and the wall. It was just wide enough to crawl along. It was also filthy, and I emerged scattering dead leaves and twigs, to belt to the block. I wondered why they looked at me curiously. I was absolutely filthy – 'Black bright!' as my mother called it.

'Farmer, farmer' was less of an effort. Someone had to stand at one side of the street and the rest on the opposite pavement. We would then all chant 'Farmer, farmer, may we cross your coloured water on our way to school?' The 'farmer' would reply 'Not unless you are wearing pink – or blue, grey, red, whatever colour the 'farmer' picked. Then you could take one stride forward if you were wearing anything of that colour. The first person to reach the other side was the winner.

It was the same with 'Film Stars'. The person who was 'on' would shout 'Roy Rogers' or 'Esther Williams', or some other film star. If your name contained any letters that were in the selected name, then you could take one stride.

These games went on for hours through the summer, and under the street light in winter, until a voice would call out 'Vaal-er-ieeee!' or 'Robiiiin!' and the named person would be hauled inside for bed, and eventually everyone would drift indoors.

'Conkers' was played in both school playground and street. Elaborate preparation went on to harden the conker before battle commenced. I would carefully knock a nail through my conkers on the back step, then bake them in the oven. It was also said that soaking in vinegar did the trick. If your conker broke the opponent's conker, then it was a one-er, if you then went on to break another, it became a two-er, and so on. If yours was a five-er and it broke, for instance, a two-er, then your conker became a seven-er. The playground became a conker graveyard with split conkers scattered around, and conkers ricocheting from walls and the floor. When conkers were no longer obtainable, the season ended and the games would peter out.

Another popular game at school was 'Husky-fusky'. There were two teams. One team would stand a boy against the wall, then in turn, in a line, the rest of the team would bend over, clutching the boy in front, forming a line of backs. The other team then ran up, one at a time, leaping as far onto the line of backs as possible, until they were all astride. The ones on the top would then shout 'Husky-fusky, finger or thumb?' holding up the required digit for the team underneath to guess. If their guess was correct, then the teams changed roles. When this happened the whole lot would collapse with a groan.

This game was stopped when a boy took a run up, jumped, and the team forming the back took a step sideways – you can guess the rest!

In winter we would congregate under the small iron street light and decide on a game. 'Hiddy' was best in the dark, creeping in shadows, surprising householders who, as they tried to get out, met with small boys crouched in their gateway.

The games were not learned but rather absorbed through the pores! These were only some of the ones we played: 'Kiss-catch'; 'Tom Tiddler's Ground'; 'Mr Wolf' and innumerable chasing games, all seemingly lost in the past. When did you last see children absorbed in one of these games in the street? A whole sub-culture has disappeared, smothered by the big hype, by television and videos; by promotion of one instant pop or sports hero after another; by constant pressure to buy, consume, wear the right product – and childhood has become the worst for it.

The rhymes and sayings echo down the past. We'd 'cross my heart and hope to die' if swearing to keep a secret. We'd ask, 'I knew three monkeys, one's called Doh, ones called Ray, what's the other called?'

And the skipping rhymes:

Each peach, pear, plum
I spy Tom Thumb.
Tom Thumb in the wood,
I spy Robin Hood.
Robin Hood in the cellar,
I spy Cinderella.
Cinderella at the ball,
I spy Henry Hall.
Henry Hall at his house,
I spy Mickey Mouse.
Mickey Mouse in his cradle,

I spy Betty Grable.
Betty Grable is a star,
S – T – A – R

Phew – and they'd keep these up for hours.

The greengrocer would trundle down the street each Friday, with a lorry made like a market stall with a tarpaulin cover. He would serve housewives under hissing white lights and my mother would sometimes buy me a pomegranate, an unsatisfying fruit, full of seeds which had to be spat out all the time.

Friday was also the evening that the *Co-op* delivery van would call, dropping off cardboard boxes of groceries at selected houses. My mother would fill in her order earlier in the week in a small notebook, and the shop would deliver. As I've said before, they always seemed to get it wrong and unknown items such as black twist tobacco would turn up in the order that I would have to take back on the Saturday morning.

Unlike today, there was no weekly 'big shop'. Food was bought daily, there were no refrigerators, no supermarkets. People were served individually at counters – sugar was weighed by the pound; butter cut from large blocks and patted with wooden paddles; and bacon sliced by a large rotating blade.

Meat was kept in a 'meat safe' in hot weather so the flies couldn't get at it. This was like small rabbit hutch with a perforated metal grille on the front. Milk was kept in a tall earthenware crock filled with water. Although we shopped at the *Co-op*, there were many other 'general' stores – *Ringtons*, the *Globe Store* and *Lipton's*. Hardware shops were crammed with items and you bought nails by the half-pound.

Greengroceries were usually bought at Doncaster Market on Saturday afternoons – enough to last the week.

Sweets were still 'on ration' in 1950, but my Uncle Barry worked as a lorry driver at Parkinson's sweet factory in Doncaster, and I'd sometimes receive a few extra from him. After sweets came 'off ration' in 1953, the newsagents where we used to wait for the school bus would be crammed with kids eager to buy as many sweets as they could afford.

The local *Co-op* was a large square shop with counters down each side. Dairy products, meat and bacon were served on the right-hand side and groceries on the left. Biscuits were displayed in boxes with glass lids, and the shop smelled of a mixture of bacon, cardboard, soap powder and other unidentifiable odours. You had to queue at the brown polished counter to be served individually and the shop always seemed to be packed. It seemed to take forever. Over on the bacon counter, a large machine with a handle would pass the bacon back and forth in front of a rotating blade. Assistants with wooden paddles would pat, shape and wrap butter; sugar was packed in purple two-pound bags. There were no supermarkets, every shop served customers individually. *The Maypole* had a large mirror set in the shop doorway and we would stand and raise one arm and leg in the air to get the reflection.

All the family were in the *Co-op*, and I could quote both my mother's and grandma's dividend number like some primitive good luck charm. So much dividend was paid back for every pound spent, so the 'divi' was very important. Now the numbers are lost, forgotten, but I know plenty of people who still can rattle off their own.

The large *Co-op* in Doncaster always seemed to be visited when we were out shopping on Saturdays. It was the largest shop in the town and on the front had a neon sign which said 'Dancing', which flashed from one neon design to another, so as to give the illusion of a man raising a trumpet to his lips and blowing. A musical note would flash on too when it happened. Inside were lifts run by bored-looking operators – you weren't trusted to operate them by yourself!

The *Co-op* also had a unique system for giving change. In one part of the shop, your money and 'divi' slip were put inside a tube. The shop assistant would then reach up and clip it to a wire, pull a cord and send the tube whizzing across the shop. There were numerous wires all meeting at a glass-walled box set high above the shop. A woman in this box would unfasten the tube, work out the change, put it inside the tube and send it skimming back.

Elsewhere in the store, this was done by pneumatics – the tube would be swallowed with a gulp. It would then rattle back after visiting some mysterious nether region.

On the top floor was the *Co-op* restaurant and café. This was cleared away for dancing in the evenings. A treat after shopping was to go there for tea, before lugging shopping bags off to the bus. There were no plastic bags. We took our own shopping bags, and if we needed extra carrying capacity then large brown paper bags with string handles were supplied. These string handles cut savagely into fingers, cut off the circulation, and had to be shifted constantly from hand to hand.

The *Co-op* men's shop was across the road on the street leading to the station. I was hauled there to buy such objects as caps and mackintoshes. It was all heavy brown wood and contained drawers which slid out from under the counter.

Before setting off on such a trip, which was usually the waste of a good Saturday afternoon, I was 'got ready'. The clothes I wore depended on the importance of the trip – was it just the market, or the *Co-op* as well?

I had three 'sets' – play clothes, school clothes, and my best clothes. School clothes could always be covered up with a mac, but my cleanliness was closely inspected. 'What people would say' was a powerful incentive in those days.

My mother would get me in a left arm-lock and, with a flannel and gritty soap, rub until I looked as though my face had been boiled. I would then ruefully dry my face and neck with the kitchen towel before passing muster.

I always enjoyed the market because we usually got a bag of Armitage's boiled sweets – always half a pound of 'mixed' – and it was there I could buy my *Captain Marvel* comics.

The fish market was just to the left, and I gaped at huge conger eels draped from one side of the stall to the other, and other odd fishy life – or, should I say, death.

A disproportionate part of my time seemed to have been spent in shops. Either buying 'barm' for my grandmother (barm was yeast, to the uninformed) or nipping to the *Co-op* or the fish and chip shop, or down to the beer-off on Sundays for ginger beer.

The only mystery was I never seemed to get any better at 'reckoning' my change, and I was never so sure of my ground to challenge anyone if I thought they'd made a mistake.

I lived in terror of a surprise mental arithmetic test at school; I went in terror in case I was bullied; I worried if we were having any sort of written test. Really, I was having a continuous nervous breakdown and no-one noticed.

CHAPTER 6

Haircuts and hang-ups

A HUGE PART OF MY TIME seemed to consist of acres of boredom, but then time is relative. An hour now was equal to three hours then. That's inflation for you!

Going to the barber's, Sunday School, and school holidays when everyone else seemed to have disappeared, topped the list.

It seemed I was despatched to the barber's if my hair threatened to show any kind of growth. With dragging feet, I would walk to Bernard's at the top shops. The shop was always full and was lined with old pub benches, with one solitary chair with arms. It was always my ambition to sit in this chair, but I never did.

The shop had a row of fidgeting, pushing boys, who were always being told to behave or get thrown out. Small tables held a raggle-taggle pile of comics and magazines, and I would gingerly edge one out to read.

The snag with this was that you could easily lose your place, so a constant eye had to be kept on who was next – more anxiety!

There were no blow waves then, or unisex hairdressing – you got a short back-and-sides and liked it! The talk was always of football, and how Doncaster Rover's had got on, and didn't someone think that so-and-so had had a good match?

The wireless always seemed to be sounding the pips for the six o'clock news, and 'Brylcream' adverts featured Denis Compton.

The wait seemed agonisingly slow and although the two barbers went at it with a will, the shop never seemed to empty. The comics were always a disappointment too, with vital pages missing.

When I did eventually get in the barber's chair and was swathed with the cloth, I was consumed with more anxiety. As my locks fell about me, I always went into terminal decline because I thought he was cutting too much off and I'd look ridiculous. I'd look like certain boys at school with hair cut close to the skull, and a violent blue paint applied here and there. I was always too timid to tell him to stop.

'Anything on?' he'd ask, and at a nod from me, he would plaster my hair with a thick green liquid kept in a big bottle. Rubbing it in vigorously, he would slip out his comb and I would finish with a fierce parting as straight as an axe blow. On the way home, this liquid would dry and I could then lift my hair like a lid, hinged at the parting. Hair was then meant to be stuck down and my mother also had a patent preparation into which she would dip a comb before administering to my tonsorial elegance.

As we were 'Chapel', I was despatched to Sunday School most Sunday afternoons. I tried every way I could to get out of it. Staying out in the garden, hoping my mother would forget the time sometimes worked. Pointing out it was raining and I'd get pneumonia also worked sometimes, but as like as not, I would be stuffed into my best clothes and sent off to the Chapel, down the bottom village.

Sunday School was held in the hall attached to the side of the Chapel. The hall had a wooden floor and dust motes would drift lazily in shafts of sunlight. We would sit on wooden benches with backs which could be swung to point one way and then the opposite.

It's about here my memory fades. I know we sang hymns and were then despatched to classes according to our age. Our class was taken by a grumpy individual, and we would sit around a stove smelling strongly of coke fumes, but what he said I have no idea. My theological education seems to have become blanked out.

We would then congregate back in the large room with the stage at one end and sing more hymns, receive a homily and then be released. The joy of escaping this torture can never be experienced again. I'd burst from the doors, and with legs pumping, shoot up the road opposite, down the jennel against the *Royal Hotel* pub, and with breath panting, slow to a jog home.

I would always run if I got fed up with walking, trail fingers against brickwork or rattle sticks along fences, leap up to snatch leaves from low branches, or walk with one leg in the gutter and one on the pavement, pretending I'd got a bad leg.

Sundays were always such long, boring days, and always followed a set formula. I would get up to a breakfast, cooked by my Dad, of bacon, egg and tomatoes, and then my Mother would set about 'getting the dinner on'.

Sometimes Dad and I would go for walks while dinner was prepared. We walked in winter and summer. In winter our heels echoed along frosty lanes, while the fields lay hard and brown on either side. In summer, I would fell cow parsley on the roadside with a whirling stick. I was the finest swordsman in France, actually putting out candle flames without hitting the candle, or despatching enemies with a gay laugh and a flashing blade.

The usual route for walks led past my old infants' school with its fresh smelling flowering currant bushes – welcome relief after passing the allotments with their fresh smelling pig sties! Up the hill, the lane went out into open countryside. Walking was looked upon as a pleasure and whole families would go for walks, especially on Sunday evenings.

If we didn't go for a walk, I would be sent to pay the 'Druids'. No, my Dad wasn't a tree-worshipper, but a member of a Friendly Society which paid out so much a week if he was ever off work ill. I would go up the road, turn left to skirt 'the triangle' and down Broomhouse Lane.

Knocking on a back door, I would be ushered into a kitchen exactly like ours and would fidget while the money was entered into the book and the book then handed back. The kitchen always smelt of roast beef, and the smell would pervade the air on Sunday mornings.

After skimming through *Reynolds News*, my next errand was to the beer-off to get either a large bottle of ginger beer, or a bottle of India Pale Ale and a lemonade to make shandy to go with our dinner.

Sunday dinner was always eaten to the accompaniment of *Two-way Family Favourites* on the wireless. This was always followed by the *Billy Cotton Band Show*, which I detested. Then, if unlucky, I was sent off to Sunday School. Sunday tea always featured cling peaches but I had to eat plenty of bread and butter first. Supper would be beef sandwiches made from meat left over from our midday meal. It was unheard of to eat out in the evenings; if you ate out at all it was either at midday or tea time.

I always found Sundays faintly depressing and even now it is not my favourite day. It only takes hearing two bars of a hymn tune and it all comes back to me – the long, long hours sat on hard benches in Sunday School, and all the words of the hymn!

Another event my parents insisted on me attending were 'Chapel Socials'. For some reason, I found joining in the various games highly embarrassing and would hang back, an eager wallflower, while laughter, bumps and bangs went on around me.

Occasionally the Chapel would have a film show and I would be eager to go to those, but for the life of me I can't remember what they showed – something uplifting, no doubt.

Also of excruciating embarrassment were the Chapel Anniversaries. There would be much banging and hammering in the Chapel itself the week before, which culminated in the erection of a steep wooden structure. The whole Sunday School would then be arrayed in their Sunday best on this platform. The tiny tots were at the bottom, and then rising up in seniority, with the oldest children up at the top, heads brushing the ceiling, and breathing through oxygen masks!

We would endure weeks of learning special songs before the event and individuals would be trained to do recitations. The Sunday of the anniversary would dawn and we would tour the streets of the village, marching behind a lorry. Perched on this lorry would be the tiny tots, jerking and rolling as the lorry inched forward. Also on the lorry was a piano. When the lorry stopped, the piano would strike up, and a hymn was sung – then we'd set off again.

I tried my hardest to look unobtrusive. I skulked behind larger boys and tried to merge into the background, in case someone saw me. Eventually I would slide off to the left as the procession went to the right – there was only so much a boy could stand!

The anniversary celebrations were held both in the afternoon and the evening. We would assemble in the Sunday School before leading off into the Chapel and clambering up the human magazine rack.

The small kids at the bottom would be led halting and stumbling through a song with their teacher mouthing the words. Then would follow a recitation from a small girl with large hair ribbons, usually delivered at the gallop, with huge gulps of breath. This was greeted with slow nods of approbation from the audience, who would smile at the person at either side of them – and, usually, they hadn't heard a word.

So the torture went on. I squirmed inwardly from embarrassment, even more so if I saw my parents sitting proudly in the audience. I had the reputation for being shy, and this was true, to a certain extent. These occasions certainly did nothing to get rid of my shyness.

Children today seem much more sure of themselves, and are more sophisticated and knowledgeable about things we had never even heard of, and couldn't imagine.

Stern warnings from my mother never to go off with anyone even if they offered me sweets, or should I say especially if they offered me sweets, were accepted. It was just another thing mothers said, like I was 'black bright', or 'don't walk in front of my feet'.

There were other churches in the village, St John's which was Church of England, and, right next to our school, the Catholic Church. This had a bell, and its tonk, tonk, tonk, could be heard at our end of the village, rising and falling with the wind. For some reason I couldn't fathom, Catholics didn't come into school assembly with the rest of us, but were despatched to the church.

School assemblies made such an impression on me that I can't remember a thing about them – even more boredom! We would be herded into the school hall, with its wooden parquet floor, and the large tin ventilator on the roof. Some of the wooden blocks on the floor were loose and could be rocked backwards and forwards while the assembly went on.

There were days when, galloping out of our passage bright with morning sunlight, I would skid to a stop in an empty street. Then followed the rounds of calling on others to see if they were coming out to play. Some would be going out with parents, others weren't out of bed, some weren't coming out at all.

Hours of unfilled time then stretched before me. I could, of course, collect old cardboard boxes together and burn them in Grandad's garden. He had a garden syringe and if you plunged it in hard enough a spout of water could be sent across the garden. I could tinker with his ancient greenhouse heating system, and get told off. I could mooch about our back garden, try knife throwing with six-inch nails or get together a ladybird circus.

This involved turning a dustbin lid upside down and filling it with water. Islands could be made with half bricks and connected with stick bridges. These could then be populated with ladybirds.

These insects were handled with affection, but others, known as blood suckers, were shunned. They could fasten on to you if the mood took them and suck your blood so that you died – or so we believed!

Butterflies were captured by having a jacket flung over them, gingerly extracting them and keeping them in an empty two-pound jam jar, held with a string handle.

We were all familiar with silverfish, which lived around the hearth and were killed with white powder.

If I complained to my mother that I'd got nothing to do, she would comment that she'd soon find something for me – thus precipitating me out in the street again.

Ah, my pals were out now, and an expedition to catch tadpoles was being organised. These were usually caught in the brickyard pond, up the street and along a rutted track. The pond lay in the bottom of a deep excavation with a curious red clay. This had the property of not only sticking solidly on shoes, but rapidly crawling up your legs and transferring itself to other parts of the body.

Butterfly nets were usually conscripted to catch the 'taddies' until everyone had a jar full, topped up with pond weed which we swore we had seen them 'chomping'.

The pond had large planks floating on it which we'd gingerly push away from shore with an outstretched leg. The rim of the hole would overhang us, like the edge of a volcano, and ragged weeds obscured large lumps of discarded clay. Over on the other side were other ponds where minnows could be caught, but these were more difficult to catch than 'taddies' and thus escaped a life of captivity.

Carrying the jar home, I'd rapidly get rid of the ladybirds and transfer my new pets to the dustbin lid. I'd then cover it with a piece of wire netting so that birds wouldn't eat them, and wait for frogs to appear. If they ever did, they must have done it in the night and then rapidly hopped off, because I cannot ever remember raising a single one!

The garden shed could also be explored if I was bored. Tins could be overturned and nuts, bolts, washers, nails, old plugs and other bits and pieces sorted through. If I was lucky, I'd sometimes find a ball bearing but these were banned, usually from marble games.

My Dad kept paint brushes in jam jars filled with water to keep them supple, but usually they dried out to hard, stiff, paralysed bristles. Garden tools hung on the wall – a fork with a prong missing, rusty hand trowels, a large file without a handle. Old tins held different sizes of nails and these could be hammered into pieces of wood, making the floor jump and dust settle from ledges and crevices.

Another period of boredom was visiting the doctor's surgery. The waiting room was T-shaped with hard padded benches around the walls where everyone spoke in whispers.

It was here, sifting through old magazines, I found stories about a curiously named individual called Captain Hornblower, and I became hooked. The stories were serialised in a magazine long gone – *John Bull* – and I would often be halfway through when we would be called into the surgery.

The usual procedure then was for Doctor Ward to hand over a prescription, which we would then take back into the waiting room and tap on another door and a hatch would shoot up. The prescription was made up there and then.

Although much of my time seems to have been taken up by boredom, embarrassment and downright fear, surely it can't have. I wouldn't be the well-balanced character I am today!

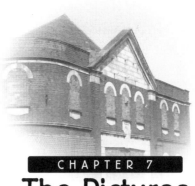

CHAPTER 7

The Pictures

O NE OF MY CHIEF PLEASURES was to go to the pictures on Saturday night with my dad. The building was a large barn of a place, with a balcony, and was at the bottom village – yet another walk!

We usually went on Saturdays, as this was classed as the 'big picture'. The films were changed three times a week, but the other two films were usually gangsters or westerns – hence one of the nicknames of the place being the 'Ranch House'. Others were less complimentary – the 'Bug Hut' and the 'Laugh and Scratch' were two, going on the fond assumption that the seats were infested with various forms of insect life. The pictures were closed on Sundays, reinforcing the gloom which descended on that day.

Built into a corner of the cinema was a tiny shop which sold sweets and huge ice lollies. For just one old penny you could get an iceberg on a stick! We always went well prepared in case starvation set in during the performance. An apple in the right pocket and a bag of boiled sweets in the other kept the hunger pains at bay.

Children weren't allowed in without an adult and would plead with anyone going in to take them in with them. There were usually kids hanging about outside the entrance, with a plaintive, 'Tek me in mister!'.

Outside were two display cases, one on either side of the door with photographs from the coming attractions. Posters distributed throughout the village also made sure everyone knew what was on. These were distinctive long, thin sheets, written with long, thin letters.

Once through the inner doors, you had to turn either left or right. The walls here were decorated in large, much retouched colour photographs of the stars. In fact I think they were black and white photographs which had been hand-coloured.

Inside, the tip-up seats were inspected for holes before sitting down. The front few rows were cheaper as, although they had tip-up seats, they were wooden. Hence, the silent multitude sat at the front would rise as the lights went down, and creep to the seats at the back. This was usually accompanied by calls of, 'I've seen you!' from the woman from the pay box who would sometimes stand at the back.

The Wedding Samba is a tune engraved indelibly on my memory. This is because the cinema seemed to have only six records with which to regale the audience while they waited for the film to start – they always played this one.

In those days you certainly got value for money. The programme would start with a travel film in black and white, so boring that people would bite the backs of seats in despair and have to be led sobbing up the aisle. (Perhaps this was a management ploy to make the rest of the programme seem good.) Next would be an episode from some interminable serial – *Superman*, *Rocket Man*, *Jungle Jim* or some other hero.

As we didn't go to the pictures every Saturday, my grasp of the plot of one of these was somewhat sketchy. *Rocket Man* concerned a scientist, who, when donning an outfit consisting of a bullet shaped helmet, heavy leather jacket, control panel and rockets strapped to his back, could fly! He always looked faintly silly dressed in this modernistic gear with his suit trousers showing beneath. Why he never suffered terminal burns to his nether regions was never satisfactorily explained. He usually foiled devious plots to steal devious formulas. These were carried out by gentlemen in large suits and hats led by a mysterious character usually wearing a mask, called 'The Dragon'. The formula was owned by another scientist who always had a young, glamorous assistant or daughter.

Superman did mostly the same sort of thing, apart from holding back cars by picking them up by the back bumper, or stopping runaway diesel locos. The crooks looked the same and probably were.

Then there was *Jungle Jim*, who could stand fearlessly against a rear projection screen showing an elephant stampede. Jungle Jim – grips like a crocodile and as entertaining as an elephant's bum. All these serials and travelogues were in black and white.

Then, to cheers (oh yes, we had audience participation), would appear a Walt Disney cartoon. In glorious Technicolor, we were enthralled by the highly-coloured antics of Mickey Mouse or Donald Duck.

We would then get the trailers for next week's offering and the adverts. During the interval, the large lady who took the tickets would walk down the aisle and stand at the front selling ice cream and huge ice lollies.

The lights would then fade and we would be regaled with the 'B-picture'. These were always in black and white and seemed pre-occupied with crime and the detection of crime. Films where police inspectors wore long macs and trilbies and drove around in Wolseley cars with radio aerials on top.

The crimes were always committed in large country houses with gravel drives, and the whole thing introduced and signed-off by Edgar Lustgarten. Sometimes, to vary it, an American would be written into a film and explained away as, 'He's over here giving Scotland Yard a hand'.

Of course, the projector would always break down sometime during the show. The soundtrack would descend three octaves and the picture flicker off. This was the signal for more audience participation, usually beginning with a groan, then hand-clapping, whistles, stamping feet, playing imaginary brass instruments, sawing wood, and generally causing a nuisance in a public place. After a while the picture would trickle back and the sound of people talking under treacle would clear, the action would start again accompanied by ironic cheers from the audience.

One of the favourite supporting pictures, which would be greeted with loud cheers, featured *The Durango Kid*. The plot so far: now in the old West, there was this ordinary cowpoke. But when trouble brewed he would ride into a secret cave, and emerge clad all in black, with a mask and cloak, on a white horse – The Durango Kid.

Thus arrayed, he would ride forth, vanquish all evil, and return to the cave to emerge as the ordinary man about the West again. No-one knew who the Durango Kid really was – but we did!

When he was humiliated in the saloon by a gang of desperadoes, led by a man with a pencil moustache and a black frock coat, we would hug ourselves with glee! Just wait! Then, as the Durango Kid burst into the same saloon, trussed up the villains with their own braces after shooting their guns out of their hands, we would explode in cheering and clapping. Many an adult seeing a small boy running along the pavement slapping his behind with one hand and holding the other in front, with a mac slung around his shoulders, secured by the top button, would have no idea they were actually seeing the Durango Kid.

Then came the 'big picture'. I was particularly fond of epics, which usually featured such stars as Victor Mature, flexing his pectorals. I would sit in the bath and examine my own chest and ponder why he was so well endowed with muscle and I wasn't.

Any film with a cast of thousands was a pushover for me. Even better if they were hitting one another with swords or wearing armour or falling from castles.

Films featuring Robin Hood would keep our games going for days, with much filching of string for our long bows and cardboard for flights for the arrows.

Dean Martin and Jerry Lewis, Bob Hope, Red Skelton, I found painfully funny. I watch them now quite blankly when they appear on television – what was all the fuss about?

Stories based on *Just William*, or the Ealing comedies would make me almost writhe with enjoyment. One thing the films did was to install certain daft ideas in our heads. If anyone got shot it was always in the shoulder.

The shoulder was, and still is in films, a safe repository for any lethal missile which happens to be flying about. Never mind that a bullet would, in reality, shred muscle; smash bone; cause heavy bleeding and instil shock – the hero would be up and about in a couple of days with his arm in a sling!

If a bullet/spear/arrow needed extracting – simple! First, if it was an arrow, it had to be snapped off. Major surgery could then quite easily be carried out on a kitchen table. Pass a bowie knife through a flame and start cutting. Disinfectant? Why, splash a bottle of whisky about. It was all done without anaesthetic, unless recourse was made to the disinfectant bottle.

If babies were about to the born, huge quantities of water were immediately put on to boil. Not that I knew what was involved in a baby arriving in the world. I always thought vaguely that babies had to be boiled, somehow this was part of the process.

American woodwork always seemed particularly flimsy. Banisters were shredded like reeds when a fight took place, chairs came apart at the slightest strain, and windows and their frames exploded outwards when hit by a falling body. American cars also had shocking steering. Think of the scenes where a couple are chatting whilst driving along. They looked at each other for long periods, and whilst this was going on the wheel was swung vigorously from side to side. Either the steering was out or they were driving on some peculiar roads. Presumably they steered by the stars, because they certainly were not looking where they were going!

Royal Navy Captains always clenched pipes between strong, white teeth; Robin Hood's men always roared with laughter, whilst clapping each other on the back; pirates wore shirts with big sleeves and there were always loose ropes to swing from in the rigging.

As the pictures were cheap, some elderly people attended every performance and gave a running commentary to their friends – one jump ahead of the action. Thus anyone sitting near them knew what was going to happen before it did.

People in the balcony had the habit of getting rid of orange peel, apple cores or lolly sticks by throwing them over onto the people below. If you watched the cone of light from the projection room, these could be seen, illuminated briefly, as they travelled onto someone's head, with outraged shouts from the person on the receiving end of the missile. It paid to choose your seat carefully.

There were two houses every evening but we always attended the first one. My mother disapproved of the second house for some peculiar reason.

There were, of course, dozens of pictures houses around. *The Windsor* at Balby, a large cinema which has since been demolished and replaced by a filling station; the little *Balby Pictures* is now a supermarket warehouse. There was the *Gaumont*, *Picture House* and others in Doncaster, and each village had their own – dozens spread around the landscape, until the late 1960s, when television began to close them down.

If a picture that we especially wanted to see appeared at any other cinema, we would hop on a bus and go there. But mostly our village cinema sufficed. I never, though, became a big fan of the movies.

If a favourite appeared, such as a film with Dean Martin and Jerry Lewis, then the picture was a must. Otherwise it was the story that mattered to me, not who was in it – *Ivanhoe*, *Shane* and *Samson and Delilah*, swashbuckling pirates, war films were all grist to the mill. I never became a movie 'buff' or appreciated the finer parts of direction.

It's not the same hiring a video – there's no atmosphere, no excitement… as the cinema grows dark and the music starts… no emerging blinking into daylight again after being immersed so deeply in a story that one becomes one of the characters.

CHAPTER 8

Dad

MY FATHER WAS A BIG MAN with bulging biceps and upper arms. He was chargehand in the boilers at the local pit, and shovelling coal into furnaces tends to lead to large muscle development.

He would come home every day and, to astonished gazes, demolish a huge 'Desperate Dan' dinner of mashed potatoes, turnips, peas, carrots, meat and very thick gravy. After that he would eat a rice pudding made in a basin, and then have a snooze.

My father had a certain habit. To put it delicately he suffered from flatulence. Well, *he* didn't suffer from it, but everyone else did! His enormous emissions were great thundering cacophonies which erupted forth anywhere. When his dinners included stuffing and Brussels sprouts, storm cones would be hoisted on the Humber! People would lash down shed roofs and small dogs cowered in cupboards as he thundered out. Windows would rattle and birds drop in flight. We would run for it and search frantically for war-time gas masks. It's not the kind of subject discussed in genteel dining rooms, no doubt, but it happened.

One of his workmates would call for him every morning, and would dance to the rhythm my dad produced all the way down the street.

I remember one occasion when we visited a local park and Father did his own thing as usual. A woman walking with her husband turned and berated him, her own husband, for being so vulgar in public, despite his protestations of innocence. We were all convulsed with laughter as my father passed by with a smile on his lips. He should have been a professional, as the Frenchman Le Pétomane was at the turn of the century. (Le Pétomane turned one of nature's foibles into a gift and had a stage act where he imitated machine gun fire, played tunes and produced other amazing noises from his rear end.)

There was one thing you could say about my dad and that was that things happened when he was around.

For instance, we were shopping one Christmas and struggling to get out of a shop against the tide of shoppers coming in. My father suddenly drew himself up to his not inconsiderable height and, pointing, said loudly, 'All that way round, please'. The crowds slowed, stopped, turned around and went back the way they'd come – and we simply walked out of the shop!

On another occasion, we were playing football on the beach at Scarborough during the summer. I was in goal, and Dad and a few others were shooting the ball at me. He came in with a devastating shot, I made a dive and missed. I lay there on the sand and watched the impossible happen. A large man had just bought a *Jaconelli's* ice cream, the sixpenny variety – huge piles of ice cream in a giant cone. He had seated himself in a deckchair, opened his mouth, when the ball bulleted past, whipping the ice cream off the top of the cone, as close as was possible. It happened so quickly, he took a lick of thin air!

The man was furious, claiming my dad had done it deliberately, but as Father pointed out, quite reasonably, he couldn't have done it again if he tried a million times. He gave the man the money to buy another ice cream. And as the story spread they were wheeling oxygen tanks onto the beach to revive holiday makers who were still weak with laughter.

Another incident involving an ice cream happened at Bridlington, on one of those holidays when there's rain every day. We had given up and gone to an awful afternoon seaside show. 'Uncle Sid' was performing. Now, Uncle Sid was a clown, and he was going around the audience sitting on ladies' knees and kissing them – obviously as much to their disgust as his enjoyment.

All the dads had had to stand up, for some reason, and mine was standing there eating a tub of ice cream, when Uncle Sid arrived in the row in front. He settled himself on a woman's knee and was just about to kiss her when my dad quickly interspersed the tub of ice cream between Uncle Sid's face and hers. He plunged his nose deep into the tub and drew back with a huge dollop of ice cream on his nose. It got the biggest laugh of the afternoon. Poor Uncle Sid was obviously angry about it, but unable show it – he was the funny man, wasn't he? It stopped him sitting on women's knees that afternoon, anyway.

My father came in with a puzzled face one evening and said that people had been staring at him on his way home from my uncle's house, and he couldn't understand it. Looking up from my book, I pointed out he'd walked the half-mile home sporting a big pink ribbon in his hair. Snatching it off, hurriedly, he confessed he'd let my young cousin Margaret play hairdressers and had forgotten about it.

He also had a vast fund of stories, all funny, and all allegedly true. It wasn't so much the stories but the way my father told them that made them even funnier.

There was the favourite one about the poacher who lived in his village. The local constabulary had been trying to arrest him for years and failed. However, a new young constable came to the village and, being keen, vowed to catch the poacher.

Tom, as they called the poacher, also had an allotment and used to spread the contents of earth lavatories on it. He collected this by lifting up the flap at the back and shovelling it into a sack. Walking along one night with the sack over his shoulder, he was accosted by the constable.

'What you got in that sack?' he demanded.

Tom refused to tell, so the policeman grabbed the sack and plunged his arm inside.

They had to move him to another village as each time he went on his beat, he was pursued by kids who would shout, 'What you got in that sack?' whenever they spotted him.

In hot weather, Dad would strip down to his vest and trousers and, looping his braces over his shoulders, sit on the front step to keep cool.

When going for a walk, on a Sunday evening, he would dress in what my mother called his sports coat and flannels, with no tie. Thus, he could put his shirt collar outside his jacket. The jacket pocket was filled with an array of pens, though he never wrote anything down to my knowledge.

He would sometimes take me with him to collect his pay from the pit. We would walk down the main road, through the village, past the pictures, then the field where the pit ponies spent their 'holidays', past the billiard hall and the *York Hotel* and on through the pit gates.

We would join a queue and my dad would receive an envelope thrust through a special window. He would open this and produce a long strip of white paper about half-an-inch wide and a foot long. This listed his wages and stoppages and was be studied intently before we went over to the pit canteen.

While all this was going on, Dad would be greeted by others he knew and I would get my hair ruffled. In the canteen we would sit and drink miniature bottles of milk, with a wide top secured by a cardboard stopper.

They held about a third of a pint.

He once took me into the boilers where he worked, and I remember being scared. I was scared of the roaring fires, the hissing steam, the clangs and bangs and thought we were much too close to the boilers' mouths for comfort! But the one time I rode on the colliery shunting engine around the pit yard was great fun.

The pit chimney, with the ladder running up the side, intrigued me. I could never conceive that anyone would want to climb such a thing or actually did, but Dad assured me that someone had to, for what reason I can't imagine.

The plume of smoke from the chimney, with a the prevailing wind, passed right over the Miners' Welfare ground. This had a cricket pitch with a pavilion. The pitch was surrounded by a red shale cycle track. There was a large paddling pool and the usual rides and swings, and also several football pitches. The ground was divided up by old colliery winding ropes cemented into thick bollards forming fences which could be swung on.

The only snag was that the smoke from the pit chimney deposited a fine soot over everything, depending how the wind blew. You had to be very careful where you sat or you became 'black bright'!

The Welfare was also on the route of one of our walks. We would come down the 'back lane' (this was actually called Broomhouse Lane), with the pit a field away over to the left. It's all built up now, but was open fields then.

Slung over Broomhouse Lane was the aerial, a ropeway upon which huge buckets of colliery spoil slowly trundled. A mesh screen protected the road from anything which fell off before the buckets passed on to the slag heap. A trigger device caused the buckets to tip over – creating a cascade of spoil which bounced down the grey shoulder of the slag heap as the empty buckets swung around the end pylon back to the pit.

Further down the lane, the old pit heap burned. I was fascinated by this, smoke rising out like a series of junior volcanoes. Sprawled over the heap were hoses which kept the fires damped down. The air reeked with the acrid smells of these internal fires, which flared up and died away. Years later, when reduced to red shale, it was used as a base for the Doncaster Bypass.

We would turn left up a narrow lane, passing under a railway bridge before turning through the Welfare gates further up the lane. My dad would watch a football match while I swung from the various swings and rides, like a monkey. Going home, we would pass through the gates at the other side of the Welfare and go back up the main road to the village and home.

As mentioned before, walking was a pleasure, and we had regular routes which we'd decide on on the spur of the moment – turning left or right at the bottom of the street would determine if it were a long walk or short, through countryside or the village. Would it be all the way to Doncaster and catch the bus back? Or just up the lane and around the village?

Sunday evenings were the times for a more staid walk. In stiff clothes, we would catch the bus to Balby, walk through Hexthorpe Flats and back by bus. Beef sandwiches for supper and then to bed.

In the school holidays I would also go out on walks with other kids from the street. We always took supplies of jam sandwiches and bottles of water, carried in canvas gas mask cases, slung around our bodies. We would set off in a straggling, pushing line up the lane, past the allotments, past my old infants school, past the three detached houses and out into fields.

Up the hill, which was bordered on one side by a very high stone wall, most daring if you climbed up and walked on it, and past the old church with its ancient drunken gravestones.

Over the stile and we were in the Echo Field. I've no idea why it was called this because there was certainly no echo. This field had two ponds and, over in one corner, the ruins of a stone tower, since demolished. Over to the left was a pollarded wood, and with sticks flashing we would lay flat swathes of nettles as we waded cautiously through these plants. We inevitably got stung, and dock leaves were immediately applied.

The wood would take up most of the afternoon. It had climbable trees, dips and hollows, and, anyway, if we got fed up there were the ponds to investigate in the field. The jam sandwiches were usually fed to surprised cows and the bottles of water thrown at each other.

We would eventually straggle home in time for tea and I would be interrogated by my mother.

'Where've you been?'
'Just up lane'.
'What did you do?'
'Nothin'.'

CHAPTER 9
Holidays

IN THE MIDDLE AGES, people didn't travel very far from the town or village where they were born. Similarly, my travel area was restricted by availability of transport and, more importantly, money.

The farthest I had probably ever travelled by the time I was ten was to Scarborough. Compared to today, with flights all over the world, and regular continental holidays on the commonplace, this seems almost medieval!

All our holidays were spent on the East Coast, Scarborough being the favourite, with Bridlington for a change, and all resorts from Skegness to Whitby ideal for day trips.

Day trips were arranged by 'someone up the street' or the Chapel. I would be awoken early and eat my breakfast in a whirl of sandwich-making and thermos filling.

The bus would pick everyone up at the end of the street, and I still know the route backwards. Through Doncaster, round the *Gaumont* corner, the odd skyline of Goole with towers and cranes, across the Humber by the bridge which always seemed to be open to let ships through.

The bus always stopped halfway and long queues would form outside the Ladies. The Gents always seemed to have been constructed from tarred, corrugated iron and the ammonia smell brought tears to your eyes.

Back on the bus, my mother would press soggy tomato and cheese sandwiches into our hands, as crunching on the gravel the bus would pull out and set off coastwards. A glimpse of the sea through buildings would cause a cascade of bags, coats, buckets and spades to be pulled off the racks.

Then it was off to 'the sands', as my mother called the beach, for the hiring of deckchairs and the staking of a claim on an area of sand. My mother always anxiously scanned the weather, would listen avidly to the forecasts, and sit in her deckchair with her coat on. She must have been the skipper on a trawler in an earlier incarnation.

But, to more important things. Wielding my spade, I would excavate the deepest hole on the beach, then sit in it. The sand thrown up could be made into a castle. Then tunnelling could start from the hole underneath this architectural triumph. I would man my fort with matchsticks – the burnt end made an admirable head.

If the weather was fine, we would spend all day on the beach, alternating between hole digging and castle making, with cricket and football on the hard sand left by the tide, and sandwich eating and ice cream guzzling.

Trailing back to the bus, after a fish and chip tea, we would sit and empty sand out of shoes, ears, bags, trouser turn-ups, hair and other odd places.

Singing would break out on the way home, led by those sitting on the long back seat. It would be getting dark as we pulled around the *Gaumont* corner and home.

My delight was a holiday in Scarborough. I thought the town was wonderful and I knew it as well as, if not better than, my home town. We always travelled by coaches run by Sheffield United Tours, lugging suitcases and bags onto the coach at Waterdale in Doncaster.

At the coach station in Scarborough, boys with box carts and handles plied for trade. Cases could be loaded on these carts and trundled to the lodge, as the guesthouses were called. We would find someone recommended by an acquaintance of my mother's, and if we liked it we would return there year after year. We stayed under an odd arrangement my mother called 'keeping ourselves'.

Thus, we would sally forth every morning and go shopping for meat and vegetables for the day and take them back to be cooked by the landlady. Then it was off to the sands with the day neatly ruled in two by dinner time, when we would all troop back. Then it was the sands again until tea time.

The evenings had many delights – a walk to Peasholm Park, where I could skin my hands rowing around the lake. Or Northstead Manor Gardens, a ride on the miniature railway to Scalby Mills and a walk back along the sea front.

We could walk right around Marine Drive and, if the sea was choppy, dodge the waves coming over the sea wall. Or it could be a trip to the Italian Gardens on the South Cliff. The permutations seemed endless.

I particularly liked the slot machine places, but these were not particularly approved of by my mother. I enjoyed the ones labelled 'The Drunkard's

Dream' or 'The English Execution'. Drop a big fat penny in the slot of a scene of a graveyard with a drunk, clutching a bottle, lying on the top of a grave, and it would whirr and click into life. Graves would open and skeletons emerge, ghosts rose up from behind gravestones, lights flashed on and off in the church, and the drunk would jerk upright and back before it shuddered to a halt and switched off.

'The Execution' showed the prisoner in his cell, being taken to the scaffold with the priest on hand, and then, with a satisfying jerk, he'd disappear through a trap door.

I would hang about so I could watch when others dropped in their penny. I was later delighted to find these in the Castle Museum at York – and still working!

The cranes were always a con, but I always had a go. Cranking the handles I could carefully position the crane jib to lower the grab on to a jumble of sweets, combs and toys which looked as though they had been there for years – and probably had! The jib would close down on a comb and on the way back to the hole it would drop it, not in the hole, but back amongst the jumble of goodies!

I never came out with any money – all that I won went back into the machines, but then that's the philosophy behind gambling. Whoever saw a poor bookie?

All our activities were, of course, dependent on the weather. My mother, in her deckchair, would keep an eagle eye on cloud formations with dire warnings of 'I don't like the look of that big black cloud' – a phrase which has gone down in our family lore. This was usually scoffed at – until one day the prophesy came true!

With a crack the heavens opened and the beach was transformed into a struggling mass of people on the run. I, and about 500 other people, crammed into the space underneath the canopy of the *Futurist Theatre* on the sea front. Meanwhile, the monsoon continued. Rain bounced back and fell again, roads were awash and, to the left, Bland's Cliff, a steep road up the cliff, was transformed into a gushing stream.

Eventually it stopped, and we were reunited with each other. My mother held her triumphant expression for days.

I didn't often don swimming trunks because I was so embarrassed at my thinness but, after nagging from my mother, I would sometimes reveal my thin body to the sun's rays and get my trunks wet. My trunks then were wool, and on becoming wet, would sag and stretch, putting a strain on the waist elastic and making my legs seemingly start somewhere around my knees.

My mother would admonish me with the phrase 'Turn your face to't sun', in hope I would return home bronzed and beautiful.

However strong the sun, the North Sea was always so cold – I fully expected icebergs to sail across the bay. After only one immersion, the shuddering would start, a blue colour would permeate the skin, and teeth began to chatter like castanets. If the weather was somewhat inclement, which surprise surprise, it tended to be, then we would have to find somewhere under cover. The pictures were always an alternative, but we also went into *Gala Land*.

Now *Gala Land* was a strange place. It was built underground. It was really a large excavation which had been roofed over, in places with glass to let the light in. It had amusements inside, such as dodgems, and booths which housed features, such as 'See the soldiers marching!' These were long lines of painted lead soldiers which were fastened down and would move along in rows as the mechanism moved.

Gala Land also had an indoor theatre with a glass roof where they held talent competitions. All the supports and sides of *Gala Land* were made to look like rock and ferns and other plants were festooned and planted to make it look authentic.

It only ever filled up when it rained, and the stall holders could be seen coming out of somnolent poses as it dawned on them they had customers.

Gala Land, sadly, is now a car park.

Sometimes I would go off on my own and explore. I'd go around the circular museum or up the hill to the castle, or in and out of the winding streets of the old town, or out on the harbour and up the winding stairs of the white painted lighthouse.

Corrigan's Amusement Park occupied the last bit of the sea front before Marine Drive started, hard under the huge castle cliffs. You could hear the music from there, and also screams as the moon rocket twirled. I didn't often venture here – my main visits to fair grounds were at home.

The fair at home in Edlington always pitched on the spare ground behind the *Globe Stores*, up the rough track which led to the bungalows. The bungalows were built of wood and painted matt black.

There was much excitement when the fair arrived and was erected. Then the call would go around the streets, 'The fair's going round!' I would cadge a few coppers and visit the raucous, generating blatter of the fair. Laconic youths would swing from dodgem cars, the 'Noah's Ark' would lurch up and down and around – but my favourite was the moon rocket.

Picture a continuous circle of closed-in cars, tilted with a life-size figure of *Popeye* in the centre. I would sit on this and whirl around until all my cash was gone; I would beg or borrow for more so I could delight in being whirled up and down, around and around. When younger, I had refused adamantly to get off and had to be physically separated from the thing.

Another must was the 'roll-a-penny', when the big flat coins were trundled down the wooden chutes hopefully to land on squares marked with different amounts of money. There would also be a boxing booth, where hopefuls were cajoled to try their luck. The light by this time would have faded, but the stalls and rides would be lit in a red and white glare from dozens of light bulbs.

The best fair was during Race Week in September when the St Leger was held. This was set up on Dockin Hill Road in Doncaster, and the lights could be seen from the other end of town.

Race Week was then always a big event in Doncaster. The town would be packed, and queues for the bus would stretch up our street past our house. Anxious-looking women would knock on our door and ask to be allowed to use the toilet.

Dockin Hill Road Fair was a monster, with at least two of everything, and side shows with two-headed calves and the 'Fattest Woman in the World'.

We would go as a family, eat saucers of mushy peas with mint sauce, buy packets of Parkinson's Butterscotch, and I could go on the Moon Rocket! Rides were three old pence, some were sixpence, but none were terribly expensive.

When the fair visited our village, my family would go on the last night, after which the generators would shut down and everything was dismantled. On my way to school I would see the waste ground deserted as it had been before, but for a few pieces of paper blowing around. The site's since been tarmacked over, and is now a car park for the local supermarket and open air market.

Dockin Hill Road is built over, and the fair, much diminished, moved to stand on the Race Course. I don't even know if it is held these days.

There was also a fair at Conisbrough. 'Ticklecock Fair' stood alongside the main road running through Conisbrough, and getting there entailed a walk over the field path, around the brickyard and down through the steep Conisbrough streets. Ever a curious child, I could never find anyone able to tell me how it came by the name 'Ticklecock'.

After digging I may have found an explanation. Conisbrough, before the industrial revolution, was an agricultural town – the largest in the immediate area. Every Good Friday, a large number of people would gather in the town to pay their tithe – a tax based on one tenth of the yearly profit of land or stock, that in ancient times had been set apart for the support of the church. Such a gathering provided the opportunity to hold a fair. The custom was to name this fair after the place the taxes were payable to – in this case, Tickhill.

Part of the merrymaking was cock fighting, so the gatherings became known as 'Tickhill Cock Fair' – which was shortened over the years to 'Ticklecock Fair' – nothing to do with amusing poultry!

They still hold the fair today, though its venue now is the Earth Centre. As a boy I remember it lining the main road through the town.

CHAPTER 10

Snow, Fun and Fireworks

THE SUMMERS OF MY CHILDHOOD were always hot and sunny, and in the winter it was guaranteed that snow would lie for at least two weeks in late January or early February. I remember waking, puzzled by the soft light in the bedroom, until it dawned on me that it had snowed!

The curtains would be ripped back to disclose a landscape transformed. Hedges and gate posts had thick caps of snow, huge expanses of unsullied white lay in gardens; roofs glistened and grey plumes of smoke rose straight against a slate grey sky. Our front path bore the footprints left by my father on his way to work, and steady flakes drove past my view.

Breakfast was a hurried meal and then I could kit myself out for going to school, first my jacket and scarf, then thick socks over my usual ones, then I would heave myself into wellingtons, fling on my cap, raincoat and gloves and straight out into the street.

The journey to school was extended by detours to walk in snow which no-one had walked on before and accompanied by exchanges of snowballs with other boys. Snowballs would hurl from behind walls and hedges; would impact with a 'clop' on house ends; would be caught and returned, and would annoy adults.

We were allowed straight into school because of the snow, and would hang around the radiators pressing on frozen, wet hands. The radiators would become festooned with sodden gloves and socks and a damp smell would hang in the air.

Leather gloves turned rock hard when dried like this and had to be hammered with a 7-pound hammer before your fingers could be inserted. Gloves became so wet through, so often, with continual snowballing, that socks were worn on the hands in their place. But these also became sodden in no time, so eventually snowballs had to be made wearing no protection at all. Much clapping under the armpits and blowing on fingers then went on in a forlorn attempt to get rid of the resulting 'hot-aches'.

Running home at dinner time and in the evening was a repeat performance of the journey to school, and I would arrive hot, panting and wet for my tea.

Then it was out into the street again. We would built barricades of snow on the pavements and store up piles of snowballs behind them, before holding huge, sprawling snowball fights.

Tiring of this, we would then roll huge snowballs, before abandoning them at the side of the road, too heavy to roll any more. But then they could be made into another barricade, or a snowman.

I always made my own snowmen in the back yard. These would wear an old hat and have eyes and buttons made from pieces of coal. A snowman was an infallible way of watching the weather. If any snow fell the depth could be gauged by the depth on the snowman, and the progress of any thaw could be noted by the slump rate, as the figure withered and lurched towards the ground.

Then, every evening, there was sledging. With the snow glistening with frost, we would stretch ourselves full-length on our sledges and hurtle down the slopes. I had a sledge, with steel runners my dad had got from work, and would pull this with a length of old washing line.

We sledged on fields sloping down to the triangle. Now covered in houses, the steep slope led to an even steeper bank, edging the road. Raincoats were discarded when sledging as, panting up and down the slopes, we became so hot, steam escaped from shirt collars. The only snag was that a ninety degree turn had to be executed at the end of the run, otherwise it was down the bank and on to the road.

All these activities were carried out in darkness, but the tall, iron street lights, reflected by the snow, gave enough light to sledge.

Magnanimously, I would occasionally allow lesser mortals to borrow my sledge for a ride. I could then judge its performance before it was dragged back by a small boy with tongue lolling, panting like a dog. And all this went on while wearing short trousers!

Another activity was making a slide or, as we called it, 'a slare'. We would make long glassy ones in the school playground. Boys would hurtle down the icy strip, balancing with outstretched arms. Back home, we'd make them on our street pavements. That is, until outraged housewives cut-off from civilisation by vast tracts of icy wastes, would remedy the situation by tipping a bucket full of hot ashes on our handiwork. We would go off muttering and make another one further up the street.

I would watch the sky willing more snow to fall and would listen avidly to the weather forecasts on the wireless. Bloated orange suns would loll in the sky before darkness fell and a hard frost would freeze any thaw that had taken place. A couple of inches of snow on top of this was, of course, ideal.

As the snow went on, the street would resound to the scrape and clang of shovels as paths and pavements were cleared. But, inevitably, the thaw would come, and the snow would dwindle, leaving black-speckled strips hiding under hedges until, eventually, these too would disappear.

The year then stretched before me arid and uninteresting, nothing to look forward to, just school and Sunday School with the oases of Saturday and Sunday to work towards in the week.

The biggest events were holidays – Bonfire Night and Christmas. Bonfire Night was planned for weeks in advance. The materials for bonfires were chopped, dragged, sawn, pinched, hoarded and gloated over. My cousin Paul furnished the site of a bonfire because their garden was bigger than ours. It never failed to astonish me where all the material came from to put bonfires together year after year.

We would scour back gardens, hedge bottoms, waste ground and the countryside to gather wood. Blunt axes borrowed from garden sheds were wielded by inexpert hands. Gangs of boys could be seen dragging piles of hedging with the inevitable length of old washing line. Bonfires would gather height on pieces of waste ground and would be guarded hard into the night.

The pressure was to build the biggest and thus the highest bonfire. Lots of brushwood was used, which added bulk but roared up in a mass of flames and was gone within minutes. What was needed were thick timbers, tyres, tree stumps – wood that would last.

Of course, fireworks, and the ways and means of buying them, were on my mind for weeks. Every penny I could scrape together went on fireworks. When you could buy a banger for a penny, and there were 240 pennies in a pound, you were rich with five shillings! We would listen with awe to apocryphal tales of how so-and-so's dad had come home with a £1 box of fireworks under his arm – £1 in those days was worth quite a bit of money.

Bangers went off with a report which turned strong men white and made dogs huddle in fear five streets away. A favourite occupation was to light a banger and put an empty tin can over it. The resultant explosion would hurl the can high in the air and cause us to rock back on our heels, hair streaming backwards.

We would collect lolly sticks from the gutter and construct little houses by pushing them into the earth side by side, adding a flat roof. Insert a banger and light the blue touch paper, retiring immediately. It would blast the construction apart and we would examine the smoking ruin with delight.

Shop assistants selling fireworks would grip the counter in frustration, baring their teeth and howling as a small grubby kid with sixpence to spend would deliberate long and hard on which ones to choose, changing his mind, and causing the assistant to have a nervous breakdown.

My favourites were bangers and roman candles, but there were jumping jacks and rockets; squibs and golden rain; volcanoes and snowstorms, which would light up the garden like day. I kept my collection in an old shoe box and would take it out and examine each one as the collection grew.

I was warned that they wouldn't go off if I handled them too much, but the temptation was too great. I made lists of what I'd bought, examining each brightly coloured tube, avidly waiting for the great day.

Tea was a hurried affair on November 5th and I galloped to my cousin's with the box under my arm. The smoky night seemed to vibrate with excitement – some bonfires were already lit and over on the horizon a rocket would burst silently into silver rain, the resultant bang coming faintly some time after.

Of course it was over too soon – the fireworks had been let off, and the adults trooped back indoors. We would then eat potatoes we had roasted in the embers of the fire – burnt black on one side, still raw on the other. We claimed we'd never eaten anything so good! Going indoors, filthy and smelling of smoke, there was dark brown sticky parkin to eat and bonfire toffee in mouth-stretching pieces.

The morning after, bonfires still showing signs of life were fed with any rubbish that could be found. Spent rockets were discovered, lying in streets or with their sticks poking out of garden hedges. Stories were swapped, which got bigger in the telling. How a jumping jack had taken a perverse delight in following you around the garden, how a firework had exploded in someone's face, making them look like a minstrel, just like it happened in the *Beano*, and how rockets had soared higher, and bangers banged louder than ever before.

Teachers at school latched on to this excitement – we wrote essays on Bonfire Night, and painted pictures depicting the scene. These essays were invariably from the 'Then we let off a banger and then we lit a snowstorm and then we lit a volcano, and then we lit a roman candle...' school of literature.

I once saved a rocket, and waited with patience until the snow came. Going out into the freezing night I set a milk bottle in the snow and inserted the stick. The rocket went up with a whoosh trailing its golden light against the hard, star-winking sky. I'd always wanted to set off a rocket in the snow, and the exercise was deeply satisfying. There was obviously something deeply Freudian about this – answers on a postcard please!

With Bonfire Night over we then all metaphorically girded our loins for the big event of the year – Christmas!

CHAPTER 11

Christmas

PREPARATIONS FOR CHRISTMAS started with Grandma making pounds of mincemeat and putting it into jars, and seemingly dozens of puddings. The puddings – in basins, wrapped in cloth and tied with string – would be put away in cupboards, presumably, like fine wines, to improve with age.

As mentioned before, I would 'help' with the preparation by stirring these mixtures with a large wooden spoon in an earthenware pancheon. It was really a cover for pinching sultanas and raisins, and for scraping out the pancheon.

At school we would be set to work making paper chains and paper lanterns. These efforts, liberally daubed with white paste, would be eventually hung across the classrooms.

Shops would begin to dress their windows, and this would start off my cajoling for us to get out the Christmas tree and decorate. My mother held out as long as possible but eventually the tree would be heaved out of the lobby-hole and set on top of the radio in the front room, in a large green pot filled with sand. We never had a real tree, in fact I can't remember any being on sale.

I would start to compile lists, then destroy them and start again. Of course, being the ripe old age of 10, I didn't believe in Father Christmas any more, therefore my lists weren't lit on the kitchen fire and let drift up the chimney so he could pluck them out of thin air.

Meanwhile, Christmas cake baking and mince pie production lines swung into action. My mother would fill tins with mince pies – supplies which seemed to last into the following February. Anyone not producing home-made cakes and pastries was looked upon suspiciously – 'She buys shop stuff', would have been the comment.

The chicken for Christmas dinner was still trotting around in Grandad's hen hut; no frozen chickens then – no freezers and no refrigerators. Discussions would go on as to whether we ought to have a 'bit of pork' as well. This was usually from someone who kept pigs on the allotments.

Meanwhile, back at school, the party would be organised. Mrs Garthwaite would ask for volunteers – so many would promise to bring, say, a dozen mince pies, someone else a jelly, and so on. On the day, the desks would be pushed together and we indulged in a feast I fondly imagined was exactly like the ones in the *Dandy* and *Beano*.

On the last day of term, we would trail home through the afternoon darkness, carrying things we'd made during the school year. Scarves turned out painfully slowly on small looms; paintings which had been stuck up on the class room walls; raffia mats and other assorted handiwork.

After getting in everyone's way, reading exciting Christmas adventures in my comics, examining the Christmas edition of the *Radio Times* – no television then, remember – avoiding Sunday School and playing around the street lamp, time rolled by and the great day dawned.

I would thunder downstairs early on Christmas morning to find a pillowcase propped up in the armchair in the kitchen – the fire being drawn by having a newspaper held around it by my dad, causing it to roar and burn more fiercely.

Objects in the pillowcase made exciting lumps and corners, and nothing can equal the excitement and delight of investigating the white container... the smell of new cardboard; the riffle of pages as a new book was opened; the delight of finding an item long lusted after; and the odd surprise present.

I well remember my dad proudly presenting me with a banana one Christmas. Because of the war, I had never seen one before, was highly suspicious of it, and refused to eat it!

I'd already had the usual rigmarole from my grandparents of how they thought themselves lucky if they'd got an apple and orange and a new penny in a stocking in their young days.

Of course, Christmas dinner was the best meal of the year – held at Grandma and Grandad's house. We'd have chicken – which was rarely eaten apart from at Christmas – Grandma's home-made stuffing, mashed potatoes, and the hated Brussels sprouts – wow! stand well back from dad!

He would preside over making shandy, in large glass jugs, to go with the meal. We never drank wine, it was probably too expensive. Anyway, it was a foreign drink, so looked upon with suspicion! There was never a huge amount of alcohol laid on at Christmas. Bottles of India Pale Ale, large bottles of lemonade and perhaps some bottles of port and sherry.

Grandma also catered for her other sons and their offspring. So I would sit with my cousins and dig in, all seated on a variety of dining chairs, kitchen chairs and stools.

Of course it all started again at tea time with cold pork and ham, pork pie, pickled onions, a big trifle, Christmas cake and the ubiquitous mince pies.

We would play games during the evening – simple ones like musical chairs – and grow hot and get silly.

On Boxing Day we would have another Christmas dinner, but this time at home cooked by my mother. Then we would get the front room ready for the visit of my Auntie Miriam, Uncle Arthur and my cousin Brian. I always liked Brian visiting our house, as he was older than me and could play the trumpet.

My dad would, first of all, carefully prop open the door from the kitchen to the hall, and the front room door. Then he would shovel burning coals from the kitchen fire, and with continuous calls of 'Mind, mind', swiftly carry it through and dump it in the fireplace, leaving a long trail of smoke behind him. More coal was added, and we soon had a good blaze. Of course all the cards on the sideboard would have fallen down again and have to be set upright – this was a continuous chore throughout Christmas. I would hang on to the cards afterwards, as they could be unfolded and afforded good areas for drawing on.

After this visit the impetus would seem to die down. There were still Christmas goodies around – satsumas, and dates in a wooden box with rounded ends; sweets in the compartments of my selection box; stuffing to accompany our dinner; nuts to crack and their shells thrown onto the fire; and the inevitable mince pies.

My dad would light a fire in the front room every morning and I would lounge on the settee with my new annuals in between listening to the wireless.

New Year was always something of an anti-climax. I always thought it was a vain attempt to keep Christmas going just a bit longer, and, in my estimation it failed miserably.

After New Year everything was cleared away. The decorations came down, the cards collected up, and the Christmas tree went back in the lobby-hole upstairs.

Then the cleaning would start, with me roped in to dust if my mother was particularly stiff. Then the front room door was closed. Christmas was over – official!

I was left with the fag end of the year, all festivities done with, a few days left of the holidays, and a whole bleak year stretching ahead until another Christmas.

But there was something to look forward to – the snow! No matter what my comics showed, no matter what was described in my books, in real life it never, ever snowed at Christmas.

Cleaning and housework seemed to be a constant preoccupation of my mother. The first job in the morning was to 'do the hearth', washing it down, then wiping it dry. The kitchen was cleaned regularly, with all the carpets coming up and the floor mopped.

Then the beds. These were made every morning – there were no duvets then – with the sheets stripped back and straightened, the blankets put back and tucked in, and the quilt arranged on top. The weight of blankets increased in relation to the temperature falling. Very small people could be entombed for days, too weak to lift the blankets to get out of bed.

My mother was always mending socks. Because all socks then were wool, inevitably holes appeared in the heels. There were no nylon ones to be discarded when a hole appeared. She would get out her sewing box and insert a wooden object, which looked like a mushroom, inside the sock so she could darn it. I would rummage through her button tin while she found and threaded the wool across the gap. As all socks were grey, matching the wool was no problem.

Washing day I disliked, especially in winter when damp clothes were hung on a rack suspended from the kitchen ceiling. This could be raised and lowered by a rope attached to a cleat on the wall. It would be so damp, I expected rainbows to form across the kitchen!

Washing clothes took literally all day. Dirty clothes would have been put to soak in a metal tub and bashed with a posher. This was either wooden with a T-handle at one end, like a spade, and three legs on the other, or a broom handle with a copper 'cup' with holes in.

One or other of these contraptions was brought down vigorously on the clothes, bashing out the dirt. Other clothes would be rubbed by hand on a washboard – which had a corrugated surface – with a large cake of green kitchen soap. Then, when the clothes had been rinsed, they would be passed between the rollers of a mangle which squeezed out all the water. Every garden would have its row of washing cracking in the wind each Monday.

Then followed the ironing. My mother would spread out an old blanket on the kitchen table and fill the kitchen with steam – piles of neatly ironed clothes would eventually appear.

Food and the preparation of food was also looked upon as very important to the status of a housewife. Very few buns or cakes were bought – my mother produced these from the oven at the side of the fire. It was also important that dinner was ready when the man of the house came home from work.

It was all good rib-sticking stuff; meat and potato pie with an egg cup inside to support the crust; thick stew and dumplings – the dumplings so light they had to be held down; large apple and blackberry pies, baked on plates especially kept for this chore; and of course, mince pies to fill up the odd corner.

In those days it was the woman's responsibility to run the home, and the man's to go to work. Some may throw their hands up, but that's how things were – no women's lib!

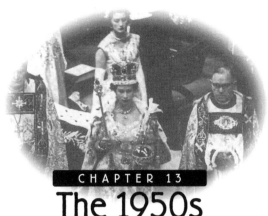

CHAPTER 13

The 1950s

IN 1950 I PASSED THE ELEVEN-PLUS and went to Maltby Grammar School. My parents had been sent a list of what I needed and I was hauled off to Doncaster to buy these essentials, to a shop in the market place, now no longer there, which seemed to be the only place where we were able to buy them. Thus on my first day I would have been wearing a brown blazer reaching to my fingertips so I could 'grow into it', a brown and yellow cap and the usual grey trousers, shirt, pullover and socks.

The blazer pocket was adorned with the school coat of arms featuring the symbols of the four houses – Barts, Rollestone, York and Bede. On my right shoulder was my new satchel in stiff shiny leather with straps and an outside pocket. In this was an old St Brunos tobacco tin containing pens and pencils.

My new football boots I tied together by their laces and hung from the satchel. I took them just in case they were needed. Kids don't have satchels these days but have huge rucksacks.

We were bussed the four miles to Maltby every morning and of course back home at night. Morning rides had boys feverishly copying someone else's homework, doctoring it to look like their own.

We had been regaled by the older pupils of tales of when it had snowed so hard the bus couldn't get through. When it did snow we watched with bated breath if this would happen again – and it nearly did!

We had waited for the bus as usual while the already thick snow got deeper. We were just trailing off home, when it arrived from the opposite direction and a teacher leaped off to round us up. Boys dove over walls, behind bushes and made other attempts to escape but I was included in the ones captured. We eventually arrived in school halfway through the morning and were sent home early, so the whole exercise seemed futile. But it made an interesting day.

The little I remember of my first day was of confusion, and being chivvied back and forth. The school was in my eyes, huge, and had an upper storey. The classes were also mixed, though girls sat on one side of the classroom and we the other.

We had a timetable given to us and mysterious subjects such as Biology and Geography, French and Physics written in. Books were handed out and instructions given to 'back' them.

For the first time I had to stay for school dinners, an experience not to my liking, when older boys divided up bowls of potatoes and meat pie and slid plates down the table – all very unappetising.

By 1953 – Coronation Year – I was an old hand. My blazer had long gone – they went threadbare in a term and were expensive to replace. My satchel had lost its shiny 'as new' look, which had not been enhanced by a bottle of ink being spilled inside it.

I had fascinated my maths teachers by my total inability to grasp the subject. They actually tried to teach me trigonometry, algebra and geometry!

I enjoyed English and used the school library a lot to borrow books. Art was now a proper subject but sport as described elsewhere was an anathema. Biology was all right, but chemistry and physics to my mind were too much like maths! French too I didn't like.

The head teacher, Mr Rush, was a red-faced rotund man who wore spats, and all the other teachers had revealed their eccentricities.

There was the history master who would hurl the first thing that came to hand at any pupil not paying attention; the head of girls who awould have been at home running a prison; and the maths teacher who would pick up a chair and point at the board with one of the legs.

In 1953 too, the Duke of Edinburgh visited Edlington Pit. Those of us from the village were rounded up and bussed home from school early for the occasion, so we could line the route and cheer as he went by. We were dropped off outside Hill Top Infants School, with only a vague idea of the role we were supposed to play. We formed what you would hardly describe as a cheering mass – perhaps two dozen kids straggled along the roadside.

We stood. Nothing happened. A man went by on a bike. We gave him an ironic cheer. We stood, hands now firmly in pockets. Nothing happened. A large black car swept by. We couldn't see anyone inside, so we did nothing.

Then the penny dropped! That was him! Not the most positive experience – but at least we got out of school early!

Strangely, lighting columns were erected in the pit yard especially for the visit – which was a bit of a puzzle, as he came during the day!

Coronation day in June, later that year, was a complete washout – literally!

Plans were made so that all the kids on Carr Road could eat outside in the street. This was hastily cancelled – to say it rained is an understatement!

I joined the throng in someone's front room to watch the coronation ceremony on a tiny 12-inch black and white television.

Watching the television was an occasion in itself in those days. The set was usually housed in a tall cabinet, and when not in use covered with a cloth and a vase of flowers or an ornament of some kind. There was only one station then – the BBC. *Children's Hour* started at 5 o'clock, then broadcasting closed down until 7 o'clock and continued until final closedown at 11 o'clock. Not many families had a set, but on special occasions you were usually invite to watch in the home of someone who had.

We watched in semi-darkness behind closed curtains. Figures came and went all day, stumbling over people in the gloom.

Meanwhile, the rain continued to pour!

No street party for us that day. I ate my meat and potato pie dinner in the kitchen of a house at the bottom of the street. The rest of the day fades from my memory.

CHAPTER 14

Edlington today

I LIVED IN A WORLD where children played freely in the streets; where you could buy metal snap tins and dudleys from every ironmonger (a dudley was a flat, circular container made of metal, with a shoulder strap, used for carrying water down the pit); where women didn't smoke – at least not in public; and fogs were so thick that standing on one side of the road, you literally couldn't see the other.

I'd never heard of a pizza, never mind eaten one. I'd no idea what an estate agent did, although I liked looking at the miniature houses they displayed in their windows.

I went back to the village in 2002 and parked my car on the land opposite the top club. This was where the fair used to stop, but it's now been tarmacked over. The road to the bungalows – now long gone – is also tarmacked over. Throughout my childhood this had been an unmade road.

Then there was the smell I hadn't smelled for years – the smell of coal smoke coming from a chimney. Walking up Dixon Road backs, chimneys were pouring out thick smoke, and, as in years before, passing gates brought huge barking hounds crashing at the woodwork. As a boy, dogs would run up to me and bite my ankles before running away.

The brickyard, instead of being a hole, is now a hill! It's been used as a landfill site and so has the railway cutting which runs alongside. This has caused the old iron bridge to become level with the ground. All the buildings are gone and the chimney has been felled.

I walked round the top of Dixon Road backs, where walls have been demolished to allow residents to park cars in their back yards, and to the top of the street where I used to live. They've driven another road between the houses, and another estate has been built in the fields at the back.

I walked down the street, past houses where the girls and boys I used to know lived. The 'Square', where we used to play so many games, is surprisingly smaller than I remember, and cars park on either side.

The houses are the same, except many have been 'improved' – plastic doors and new windows. Although many windows have been replaced in some, the old steel ones with their small panes still remain in others.

The house where I used to live has seen improvements, but the windows are much smaller than I remember. They've knocked a gate in the low wall so that a car trailer can be backed in, but the dark, glossy-leaved privet is still there, that as a boy I used to hack away at with blunt clippers.

Walking down the main road, I passed the other end of Dixon Road – and the fronts of some of the houses had been 'improved'. The 'top shops' are still there, but there's now a market on the spare ground opposite where my car is parked, and there's a ramshackle garage which seems to have been built in an absent-minded fit.

The Crown Stores were boarded up for a time, but still had the original cut-out wooden lettering above the windows. I used to buy yeast ('barm') there for Grandma. Recently it's become a hairdressers. *Bernard's*, the barbers where I spent so many boring hours, is gone, and the shop is occupied by a furniture dealer. The chip shop is a Chinese take-away; but the beer-off is still there, though the end wall, where it used to say 'Hardy's Kimberley Hansons' has long been painted over. No, I don't know what it meant either.

Past the *Royal Hotel*, now tarted up, and down to the 'bottom village', where houses have 'For Sale' signs sagging in front gardens, and the British Legion flag is at half-mast, as though it had never been taken down.

The hardware store which had two iron petrol pumps outside, is now a dental surgery; there's the ubiquitous video shop; but the Post Office across the road is still exactly the same.

The *Co-op* is now a supermarket and above it, the *Co-op Hall*, where I used to accompany my mother to meetings, has had its windows blanked out. An estate agents' occupies the shop where my mother used to buy wallpaper; houses built on what we called the 'New Estate' are going for £37,000.

Now I stood and puzzled at the library. It's much narrower than I remembered. They've put in stairs at one side of the room, leading to a separate children's library, and have knocked a wall out at the back, making it much larger. The floor is covered in carpet tiles. There are tables and chairs, unknown in my day, and a reference section.

Where they used to fill up the coal lorries for the home delivery service, there's now a supermarket. The cinema building is still there, with the date 1920 above where the doors used to be; but these are now bricked up, and it looks like it's used as a warehouse.

The field opposite where the pit ponies ran and jumped is now a filling station, and the long billiard hall is occupied by a double glazing business.

But the pit has gone.

The original gates still hang on their original posts but all the buildings, the winding gear and chimney have gone. There is a splendid new entrance just further down the road and an estate of brand new detached houses has been built on the site.

Staveley Street, which leads away from the pit gates and is the oldest street in the village, now has elaborate parking bays and trees, 'For Sale' and 'Sold' notices, and those plastic front doors. Cars park on either side, as on all the streets, it seems, these days.

Then there is the school – Victoria Road Junior School. Gone are the outside lavatories and the air raid shelters, and there is a gate in the wall now leading into playing fields at the back. The steep roof still has the pointed ventilators on top. I ran my hands over the brickwork where we used to climb over the school wall at home time. It's still chipped and worn from all those schoolboy antics all those years ago.

The 'Rec' is now graded, and has neat football pitches where groups of gulls stand waiting for something to happen. The surrounding fence, once made from old sleepers, has been replaced with a chain link fence.

Although, physically, much remains the same, Edlington village has witnessed many changes over the years. I was surprised I not to have seen a single face I recognised. But life there, as I remember it, revolved around the colliery and when that closed I suppose many will have left to find work and build new lives elsewhere. And the place seemed much smaller than I remember.

In 1950, when I was ten, the pit, for all its dirtiness and danger (some things we don't miss about the 'good old days'!) formed the heart of a lively community. I grew up in an environment full of warmth – not only physically warm, but spiritually. No matter how alien the outside world proved, back home we felt safe. I'm not sure how many people would say the same of their homes and lives today.